THE
MAGNIFICENT
MISSISSIPPI

Acknowledgements: John M. Zielinski, who compiled the photographs would like to acknowledge the cooperation of the staffs of the Iowa State Historical Society, Iowa City; the Putnam Museum of Davenport; Augustana College Library, Rock Island; and the Buffalo Bill Museum in LeClaire, Iowa for their help in locating photographs and other illustrations in this book.

Special thanks to Patrick J. Costello
          Costello's Old Mill Gallery
          Maquoketa, Iowa for permission to use his
          sketches from "Legends of Our Land."

Thanks to Roger Menken, Sutherland Printing staff artist, for cover art work and book design. Also to Linda Lohse-Dagel, a calligrapher par excellence for her cover lettering.

ISBN Paperback Edition 0-910381-07-0

Typography, design and printing in U.S.A. by Sutherland Printing Co. Inc., Montezuma, Iowa 50171

□

▪ THE ▪ MAGNIFICENT ▪ MISSISSIPPI ▪

Text by Jim Arpy

Photographs compiled by John M. Zielinski

▪

PUBLISHED BY IOWA HERITAGE GALLERY/PUBLICATIONS
P.O. Box 426, Grinnell, Iowa 50112

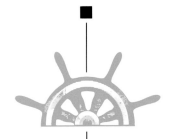

TABLE OF CONTENTS

The Purpose of This Book   7

The Great River Road   8

When Dawn Comes to the Big River   11

Mississippi Backwaters as Primitive as
Yesteryear   12

Mark Twain's Love Affair with the
Mississippi   15

End of Black Hawk's Eden   18

A Forgotten Battle   26

Handshakes and a Massacre   28

A Future President Loses a Battle on the
Mississippi   30

'Pay Up—or Else!'   32

They Named a River   34

A Wild and Wacky Voyage   36

End of the World   38

Legend of the Lovers   41

Chief's Revenge   42

'Take Command, Capt. Lincoln!'   44

Iowa's First Surgery?   46

He Married 'Minnehaha'   48

That Strange Election   50

A Bishop and a Prince   53

'Land Grabbers Keep Out'   54

Wars of Wildcat Wilson   56

A Pioneer Christmas   58

First Duel in Iowa   60

Get Off My Roof!   62

Three Killers Die   64

Rev. Hummer's Bell   66

A Four-Mile Painting   67

The Grey Eagle's Great Race for Glory   71

The Prophet's Downfall   74

A Magnificent Excursion Up the Mississippi   76

Nightmare Brought Locomotive   79

He Wouldn't Stay Hanged   81

John Brown in Davenport   82

Ghosts in the Clock Tower?   83

All Aboard the Stage!   85

Death on the Arsenal   87

Remarkable Annie Wittenmyer   91

Lansing's Last Run   94

The Big River Floods of Long, Long Ago   96

The Great Ice Gorge of 1868   101

Rough and Ready Raftsmen   103

Burlesque in Davenport   107

'Banish the Brute'   108

'Here Comes the Circus!'   109

Circus Brought Electricity   111

He Sawed Their Horns   112

Beware the 'Kissing Bug'   114

'Buffalo Bill' Cody   115

'Cut Down Those Poles'   119

Midwest Not Immune to Earthquakes   120

Honor to Fort Armstrong   122

Davenport's 'Space' Shot   125

Music, Dancing Aboard the Colorful
Excursion Boats   126

Bugging the Mayor's Office   128

Rebirth of the Father of Waters   130

Sarcophagus of Sand   134

THE PURPOSE OF THIS BOOK

No portion of the United States is more rich in history than the Mississippi Valley. Across this frontier stage marched men of destiny—Abraham Lincoln, Zachary Taylor, Robert E. Lee, "Buffalo Bill" Cody, and many more. And there were the plain folk who fought against the wilderness and won— the doughty steamboat captains, the raftsmen, the traders, the soldiers, the stagecoach drivers and the settlers. No history of the area could be complete without the deeds of the Indians who were here first, and it must include their great leaders, courageous Chief Black Hawk, eloquent Chief Keokuk, the warlike "Prophet," and others.

The events recorded here are exciting, sometimes improbable, and offer a never-before-provided "behind-the-scenes" look at pioneer life in the "Gateway to the West." Information for these historical accounts has been carefully culled from many sources—official records, old newspapers, historical documents and publications, library and museum files. Every effort has been made to check and crosscheck them and to make them as reliable as humanly possible.

The purpose of this book is to make residents of the Mississippi Valley aware of their great historical heritage, and to serve as a guide to visitors. It is hoped it will remind each of us of the debt we owe to those who came before. □

THE GREAT RIVER ROAD

Photo by Sue Katz, Rock Island

By Jim Arpy

Here misty bluffs remember days of Twain,
   still murmur of the hiss of steam
and thunking paddlewheels spitting foam
   into the muddy water, black smoke curling,
hellbent, upbound for Prairie du Chien and St. Paul.

Here puffing diesels, truck tires drumming asphalt,
   scorn old Keokuk's stair-step locks,
rolling across the squeaking zig-zag bridge,
   smudging the locking pine arch with oily fumes,
non-stop to Chicago on the Great River Road.

Here in the drifting, flat-bottomed john-boat
   unhurried the commercial fisherman puffs his pipe
and laconically hauls in his trot-lines
   moving on with a feeble, seven-horse putt-putt
in the long afternoon on the big river.

Here the little red sports car, fresh-polished
   dips and snarls down the winding hill,
stopping beneath the spreading willows
   with rasping brakes and whorling dust
while the driver chunks rocks at a lazing turtle.

The old bluffs ignore such goings-on
   to whisper of other times and other things:
of Diamond Jo, and the swift War Eagle,
   of skiffs and sidewheelers and great log rafts,
of how it was when the river was young. . of how it was.

WHEN DAWN COMES TO THE BIG RIVER

Dawn touches quiet reaches of the Mississippi River with a cathedral-like majesty that speaks of how it was when you were a child, and the beginning of each long day held infinite promise.

Shades of black separate slowly from the murky waters, and just the hint of a breeze tentatively rustles the awakening willows. Almost reluctantly the mighty river throws off its velvety sleep-shroud, as a band of delicate pink, now mixed with gold and vivid violet, edges up the horizon and peeps shyly over still-shadowed trees nodding on a nearby island.

The silence is an entity unto itself, broken only by sounds not heard in the workaday world of the city, wondrous sounds of nature waking as it did in the beginning, as it will in eternities to follow.

Here, on a grassy bank, with a squirrel beginning his morning constitutional overhead, and leaping fish splatting hungrily against the water, is peace and a feeling of oneness with nature. Here is the distant silhouette of a fisherman in his flat-bottomed scow, tending his lines as his father and grandfather did before him. Here are the tiny bubbles made by minnows skimming the surface in search of breakfast, and the hoarse harrumphing of a bullfrog up past his bedtime.

There is no hurry along the big river, because tomorrow will come as today came, and the river with infinite patience will polish the wet-shiny stones at its edge, not caring whether the grinding process takes a hundred years or a thousand, certain it will still flow here for every tomorrow to come. □

MISSISSIPPI BACKWATERS AS PRIMITIVE AS YESTERYEAR

A world little changed from the time of the Redman exists in the hundreds of sloughs and backwaters and islands of the Upper Mississippi River. These lush, primitive areas are seldom seen by tourists, or even by most of the folks living along the banks of the mighty river. The sportsmen — the fishermen, trappers, duck hunters — they know this silent world of woods and waters and they walk and paddle softly there, careful not to disturb the tranquility that doesn't exist in the world "outside."

A different world this is...strangely foreign...eerily beautiful, narrow channels snaking off the main river, some boat-bottom-scraping shallow, some deceptively deep, most stump-studded and relatively undefiled by the works of man. Mile after mile they go, looping and twisting into themselves in a dizzying maze, colorfully named "Bootleg Slough," "Break Leg Slough," "Twenty-mile Slough," the names recalling long forgotten incidents.

Photo by Sue Katz, Rock Island

One poles through clear deep water, watched perhaps by an inquisitive otter or beaver, and suddenly the boat is sloshing through a watery field of gleaming yellow lotuses with platter-sized leaves. Blue wing teal waddle ponderously along a muddy bank, unafraid because this is their domain, and man, but an infrequent visitor and nuisance. The first-time traveler of these uncharted river highways would become lost in minutes, and only the river veterans can travel them quickly and safely, knowing every partially submerged log and sandbar. Sometimes sandy beaches flaunt the weathered rib bones of ancient small boats, perhaps ripped from some mooring point upriver years before. An egret, long legs dangling, will often flap gracefully across the bow of the boat, or a water snake shoot into the water from his sunning log. Here is a place of peace, and nature unmolested. □

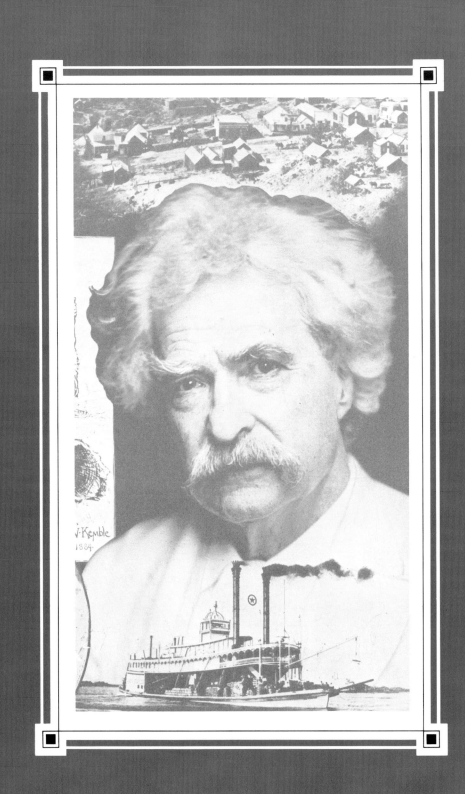

MARK TWAIN'S LOVE AFFAIR WITH THE MISSISSIPPI

All of his life, Mark Twain was fascinated by the big river, the Mississippi. Probably no man knew her better or loved her more. Fortunately for the rest of the world, Twain was more than just a riverboat pilot, though he often said he considered that the greatest station any man could attain. But because he was a writer, and a great one, he could make the river live for others, let them hear waves scrabbling against the shore, make them shiver in the cold fog that sometimes enshrouded her, and he could wrap them in her romance and gaiety and promise of adventure.

This steamboat coming 'round the bend was photographed during the latter part of the last century. The photo is one of a large collection of photos in the Buffalo Bill Museum Collection at LeClaire, Iowa.

Mark Twain loved this big, sprawling, meandering body of water, knew her sandbars and her rapids and tricky currents, and made her name a household word around the globe. Many were the tales he spun of life on the river, even as he added immeasurably to her already colorful legend.

Here are excerpts from some of Twain's writings about the Mississippi:

(Concerning the Upper Mississippi): *"The majestic bluffs that overlook the river, along through this region, charm one with the grace and variety of their forms, and the soft beauty of their adornment... And then you have the shining river, winding here and yonder, its sweep interrupted at intervals by clusters of wooded islands threaded by silver channels; and you have glimpses of distant villages, asleep upon the capes. And it is all as tranquil and reposeful as dreamland, and has nothing this-worldly about it — nothing to hang a fret or worry upon."* □ ——————

"The face of the water, in time, became a wonderful book--a book that was a dead language to the uneducated passenger, but which told its mind to me (a pilot) without reserve, delivering its most cherished secrets as clearly as if it uttered them with a voice. And it was not a new book to be read once and thrown aside, for it had a new story to tell every day." □ ——————

Cargo being loaded aboard the steamboat Dubuque in 1897. (Buffalo Bill Museum Collection.)

Lifelike bust of Twain is in the Twain Museum in Hannibal surrounded by the memorabilia of his life and work.

Hannibal, Missouri Mark Twain's boyhood home with museum and recreated law office of his father. White picket fence from Tom Sawyer surrounds small park beside his home.

Steamer Alton on the river. Collection of A & A Coins, Stamps, and Collectables, Iowa City, Iowa.

"Your true pilot cares nothing about anything on earth but the river, and his pride in his occupation surpasses the pride of kings." □————

"The Mississippi is a just and equitable river; it never tumbles one man's farm overboard without building a new farm just like it for that man's neighbor. This keeps down hard feelings." □————

"A river without islands is like a woman without hair. She may be good and pure, but one doesn't fall in love with her very often." □————

END OF BLACK HAWK'S EDEN

BLACK HAWK.

Any compilation of articles dealing with the many facets of the colorful history of the Mississippi Valley and the inhabitants of the broad and fertile area of its upper portion must properly begin with the proud and resourceful people who made the area their home long before the arrival of the first white men. For centuries, the Sauk and Fox Indians built their villages along the Mississippi and Rock Rivers, tilled the rich earth, fished in the clear waters, and hunted in the dark forests.

The heritage of the Redmen is woven inseparably into the history of the lush valley as it extends over several states, and the names he gave to rivers and places live on. Of all of the Indians with whom the white man fought, bargained, often deceived, and smoked the peace pipe, one stands out as brave warrior, eloquent orator and formidable foe - Ma-'kata-wimesheka-'ka, or Black Hawk, a fiercely independent Sauk.

Black Hawk - broken finally by his love for the land of his birth, its people and their traditions, born too early and too late. His name really meant "Black Sparrow Hawk," and, despite popular legend, he was neither an elected nor hereditary chief. He was a distinguished warrior whom some 200 braves who remained at the village of Saukenuk in 1812 followed as a war leader.

Black Hawk cherished the broad Mississippi and rich soil that fed his people, but he would see all of

▶

An Indian pictograph believed to date from the early 1830's was found between the pages of an 1840's HISTORY OF THE INDIAN TRIBES OF NORTH AMERICA by Thomas McKenny and James Hall. This copy of the book had belonged to Col. George Davenport, and was given to the State Historical Library in Des Moines where it remained unopened until 1973. This was probably an early contract given to Davenport by an Indian in order to secure supplies. He promised to hunt and fish in payment. The figure in the center tied to the hawk is said to refer to Black Hawk. This unusual find, the only surviving pictographic drawing in Iowa, is on display at the State Library.

the tribes' dominion dribble away, 50 million acres of virgin land. He would experience treachery many times over, and sometimes repay it in turn. He would meet humbling circumstances with dignity, intolerance with forbearance. Warrior, orator, statesman, Black Hawk was all of these, and though he had never read a book, his savage tongue expressed many of the sentiments of the world's most intellectual philosophers. Yet with all of his sagacity, he would be too blind, or perhaps just too proud, to read the handwriting on the wall that said it was death to the Indian to oppose the all-powerful white man.

Black Hawk was born in the village of Saukenuk, which might have been located in several places in the lower Rock River Valley. Some historians believe it was a permanent village on the north shore of the Rock River, near its junction with the Mississippi. The exact date of Black Hawk's birth was never recorded, though he lived about 71 years. From his toddling days, the shadow of death would follow and hang over him. Before he reached manhood, he would find himself inhabiting a world made dangerous by the approach of the land-hungry white settlers. Added to that was always the possibility of attacks by rival Indian tribes.

Black Hawk was just 15 years old when he accompanied his father on a raid against the Osages. He watched in awe and pride as his father slew an enemy brave and took the scalp. Then, screaming a war cry, Black Hawk rushed to an oncoming brave and drove him to earth with his tomahawk. Triumphantly, he stood over the first man he had killed, an act that in the eyes of his comrades immediately made him a brave. The tomahawk of Black Hawk would take many other lives in his lifetime, for this was a way of life, a means of survival in a harsh, hostile land.

The land over which Black Hawk and the Indians allied with the Sauk claimed dominion comprised a virtual empire and included the northwestern half of Illinois, most of Iowa, and much of southwestern Wisconsin and eastern Missouri. The village of Saukenuk had stood on approximately the same site for 150 years. In front of it, a prairie extended to the Mississippi River, and in the rear a bluff gently ascended from the flatlands.

Black Hawk, many years later in his autobiography, dictated to Antoine LeClaire, prominent pioneer settler and friend of the Indians, described this area:

"On its highest peak our watch tower (now located in Black Hawk State Park, Rock Island) was situated, from which we had a fine view for many miles up and down Rock River, and in every direction.

Drawings are by Henry Lewis from **The Mississippi Illustrated,** *published in Germany in the 1840's.*

"On the side of this bluff we had our cornfields, extending about two miles up parallel with the large river, where they joined those of the Foxes, whose village was on the same stream opposite the lower end of Rock Island, and three miles distant from ours.

"We had 800 acres in cultivation, including what we had on the islands in Rock River. The land around our village, which remained unbroken, was covered with blue grass, which furnished excellent pasture for our horses.

"Several fine springs poured out of the bluff nearby, from which we were well supplied with good water. The rapids of Rock River supplied us with an abundance of excellent fish; and the land being very fertile, never failed to produce good crops of corn, beans, pumpkins and squashes.

"We always had plenty; our children never cried from hunger, neither were our people in want. Here our village stood for more than 100 years, during all of which times we were the undisputed possessors of the Mississippi Valley, from the Wisconsin to the Portage des Sioux, near the mouth of the Missouri, being about 700 miles in length."

The village at the watch tower, headquarters for the united Sauk and Fox tribes, had a population estimated at 11,000, and was one of the largest Indian settlements in the United States.

There the Indians enjoyed a life that was, for the most part, peaceful and happy. Black Hawk loved to sit alone on his high watch tower, smoking his pipe and, in his words, "looking with wonder and pleasure at the grand scenes that were presented by the sun's rays, even across the mighty water..."

That tranquility was to be short-lived. In the fall of 1828, while the Indians were away on their annual hunting and trapping expedition, the first white settlers arrived. Trouble began almost immediately. Through the seasons of 1829, 1830 and the spring of 1831, whites and Indians quarreled over various trespasses, claimed the same cornfields, and occasionally came to violence.

Black Hawk recalled this unhappy period in his autobiography: "Bad and cruel as our people were treated by the whites, not one of them was hurt or molested by our band. I hope this will prove that we are a peaceable people—having permitted their men to take possession of our cornfields, prevent us from planting corn, burn our lodges, ill-treat our women, and beat to death our men without offering resistance to their barbarous cruelties. This is a lesson worthy for the white man to learn: To use forbearance when injured."

However, some of the whites did not report such kindly treatment from Black Hawk's people. In 1831, eight of them made this statement before a justice of the peace:

"We do swear that the Sauk Indians did through the last year repeatedly threaten to kill us for being on their ground and acted in the most outrageous manner; they threw down our fences, burnt or destroyed our rails, turned horses into our cornfields, and almost destroyed our crops.

"Further, that they stole our potatoes; killed and ate our hogs; shot arrows into our cattle and put out their eyes, thereby rendering them useless, saying the land was theirs, that they had not sold it."

There were many other charges made by the whites, including: "Nearly 50 Indians, headed by their notorious war chief, all armed and equipped for war, came to the house of Rennah Wells, and ordered him to be off or they would kill him, which for the safety of his family, he obeyed. They went to another house, rolled out a barrel of whiskey and destroyed it, as well as committing many other outrages."

Obviously it was the end of Eden. Soon blood of the white man and the Indian would spill on the rich black soil. The troubles of Black Hawk, son of Au-kenuk, had just begun. □

Drawing by Henry Lewis.

A LOST EMPIRE

Now the drums of Black Hawk spoke of war and revenge and death to the white trespasser. Gone was the peace that had blanketed the ancestral home of the Indian along the Mississippi and Rock Rivers in what is now the Quad-City area. Once the drums had told happy news—of great hunts, of brave deeds done, of marriages and tribal ceremonies. Now these times were past. Hemmed-in, harassed, harried by troops and waves of land-hungry settlers, Black Hawk and his nation stood virtually alone, pledged to save their world or die, though they had no idea of the tremendous odds they faced. They could not know it was a world already inevitably changed, a world already gone.

Without his knowledge or consent, Black Hawk had been "sold out." In 1804, a few chiefs, in return for an annuity of $1000 a year, agreed to move west of the Mississippi, ceding to the government for that paltry sum, 50 million acres comprising the northwestern half of Illinois and much of the southwestern portion of Wisconsin and eastern Missouri— land which the Sauk and Fox felt was theirs. It wasn't until several years later, though, that the first trickle of white settlers began to arrive. Probably many acted in good faith, because they came with grants to land in the new territory and they brusquely moved to dispossess the Indian "trespassers."

The government had made no move to force the Indians off the land until the settlers began arriving. But in 1830, the Indians received from the "Great White Father" in Washington, the order: "Leave your villages in Illinois and move across the river into Iowa."

It was akin to having someone tell you to move out of the house you had bought and paid for because they had purchased title to it from someone you didn't even know. Black Hawk reacted as most people would under the circumstances. He haughtily refused to acknowledge or accept terms of the Treaty of 1804, stating that the Sauk and Fox had not been a party to it, and that their lands had been sold without their knowledge.

Drawing by Henry Lewis.

Twice before, armies of the white man had come to destroy the Indian villages on the Rock River. In May, 1780, during one of the campaigns of the Revolutionary War, Col. John Montgomery of the Virginia Militia had come with a force of 350 men to burn the village in retaliation for Black Hawk's support of the British.

In September, 1814, an expedition under command of Major Zachary Taylor (later President of the United States) came to raze Black Hawk's village and destroy the growing crops. Taylor was soundly defeated at the Battle of Credit Island in Davenport by Black Hawk, numerous Indian allies, and a British battery.

Now it seemed Black Hawk had no alternative but to carry out the edict from Washington. Smouldering at the unfairness of it, he left his villages and crops and moved his people across the Mississippi into Iowa. Those who ordered the move weren't concerned that the Indians would have to leave behind their food supply, and the tribes spent the winter under famine conditions.

Deeply concerned about the starving condition of his people in the spring of 1831, Black Hawk defied the government order and moved his tribes back across the Mississippi and planted new crops in Illinois. By this time white settlers had occupied his old village and they were very alarmed at the Indians' return.

Terming it an invasion of the state, Gov. John Reynolds called for volunteers to fight the Indians. Almost immediately, 1,500 men, eager to fight Indians and protect their rights, volunteered and were rushed to Beardstown. By June 10, the militia was ready to march for a showdown against Black Hawk.

As the soldiers approached his encampment, Black Hawk sent out an emissary under a flag of truce. A shot rang out and the Indian fell dead. Black Hawk was enraged at what he considered another example of the white man's treachery, though the shot had been fired by one of the undisciplined volunteers. The war chief hurriedly withdrew his forces and began a bloody campaign of terror. Across Illinois his warriors ranged, retaking some of their former village sites and slaying the settlers.

The government moved larger forces against the Indians, and Black Hawk was forced to retreat into Iowa. Fearing he would still be pursued, and his people slain, Black Hawk went to Fort Armstrong (now the site of Rock Island Arsenal) and sued for peace. He got it—on the white man's terms. Grudgingly, Black Hawk agreed to terms of the treaty, which again provided he would stay out of Illinois.

For several months there was peace until, again driven by hunger and a desire for revenge, Black Hawk and his braves, in the spring of 1832, once more crossed into Illinois. This was the real beginning of the Black Hawk War. The Indians moved toward the Rock River, hoping to enlist the support of the Pottawatomies and Winnebagoes. The governor of Illinois called up 1,800 volunteers, among them a tall, lanky captain named Abraham Lincoln.

Under command of Brig. Gen. Samuel Whiteside, the volunteers marched to little Oquawka, Ill., on the Mississippi and then north to the mouth of the Rock River. In a few days they reached the Indian village known as the "Prophet's Town." This had been the residence of an Indian chief known as "The Prophet," one of Black Hawk's war lieutenants, and a prime instigator of the Black Hawk War. Today this is the site of Prophetstown, Ill.

Finding the village deserted, the troops burned it to the ground. Moving on to Dixon, Ill., they found two battalions of mounted volunteers, under command of a Major Stillman, waiting to join them.

On May 12, camped near a site known as "Old Man's Creek," the volunteers spotted a party of Indians on a ridge near their camp. Without orders or commanders they set out in pursuit. The Indians saw them coming and taunted them by waving a red flag as an emblem of defiance. The soldiers rode pell mell after them, unaware they were being led into a cleverly-baited trap set by Black Hawk.

When they were several miles from their encampment, the terrified soldiers suddenly saw 700 whooping braves, led by Black Hawk, swooping down on them. They fled in disorder with the Indians right on their heels. Pushing their mounts to the limit, the terrified soldiers rode right into the encampment, spreading such terror that the other soldiers also fled in chaos. Stillman tried desperately, but with no success, to rally his men, unaware that no more than 40 braves had kept up the chase. A handful of soldiers stuck by their guns and managed to route the Indians, but Stillman and his troops retreated in wild disorder all the way to Dixon. The battle, if it could be termed that, was thereafter disparagingly referred to as "Stillman's Run."

Drawing by Henry Lewis.

Though 11 of Stillman's soldiers had been killed, it was a slight victory for Black Hawk, and it would be his last one of any consequence. A short time later, he would be greatly outnumbered and defeated at Wisconsin Heights by volunteers under Col. Henry Dodge.

Black Hawk and his tribe were on the verge of starvation and were never allowed to rest as they kept trying to escape the soldiers. They fled westward, but were finally trapped at Bad Axe Creek where soldiers surrounded the Indians and slaughtered them. Though Black Hawk had often shown mercy to his enemies, his captors killed old men, women and children, as well as 150 braves. Winnebagoes, aiding the white men, caught Black Hawk, one of his sons, and the Prophet, and turned them over to the soldiers. Black Hawk and the Prophet were taken to Fortress Monroe, Va., where they were confined briefly.

Later they were released and taken on a tour of the major cities in an effort to convince them of the futility of trying to combat the people of the United States. Great crowds turned out to see them. At Fortress Monroe, Black Hawk, still the dignified leader, made an eloquent speech to the commander upon his release, thanking him for his kindness, and speaking of the land of his birth.

But even as he spoke, the hunting grounds he thought still belonged to his people were being bartered away. Six million acres of Iowa land would be sold for less than 14 cents an acre. For Black Hawk, death and even greater indignity, were not far away. □

NO PEACE IN DEATH

Though it bears his name, Black Hawk didn't sign the "Black Hawk Purchase" which agreed to the sale of six million acres of land in a 50-mile strip along the western shores of the Mississippi River for less than 14 cents an acre.

It was shortly after his capture at Big Dells, Wis., at the close of the Black Hawk War, that Gen. Winfield Scott and Illinois Gov. John Reynolds began negotiating the Black Hawk Purchase in Davenport.

The treaty was signed at Fort Armstrong (now the site of Rock Island Arsenal) on Sept. 21, 1832, by nine Sauk Indians, including Chief Keokuk, and 24 Foxes. Black Hawk was in jail at Jefferson Barracks, Mo. at the time and did not sign the document.

This was the first cession of land in Iowa. Under its terms, the Winnebago ceded all their lands in Wisconsin, and the Sauk and Fox forever forfeited their rights to theirs in eastern Iowa as "punishment" for their part in the Black Hawk War.

Black Hawk and Keokuk were alike in that both had brilliant minds and were convincing orators. But their personalities differed greatly. After the disastrous Black Hawk War, the Sauk and Fox listened to the counsel of Keokuk, who always urged compromise. He realized it was foolhardy to oppose the white man. Ever a diplomat, Keokuk had long urged cooperation with the settlers. The bloody Black Hawk War might have been avoided if Black Hawk had listened to the advice of Keokuk. Though crafty in war, Black Hawk was wary and uneasy when diplomacy was involved, preferring direct action. He combatted obstacles where Keokuk avoided them. There was intense rivalry and considerable dislike between the two powerful men. It was a hard blow for Black Hawk that the treaty spelling the end of his nation was signed not by himself, but by Keokuk.

After the treaty was signed, Black Hawk was taken to Washington to visit President Andrew Jackson. He was then ordered to return to Fort Armstrong to have read to him the terms under which he would be released from captivity.

It was a bitter blow for the old warrior to stand before his captors and be told that thereafter he must listen to his rival, Keokuk, and be guided by his counsel. A historian recorded Black Hawk's immediate reaction to the order:

"These words aroused the old fire in Black Hawk. 'I am a man—an old man,' he said in indignation. 'I will not conform to the counsel of anyone. I will act for myself. No one shall govern me.

"'I am old—my hair is gray—I once gave counsel to young men. Am I now to conform to others? I shall soon go to the Great Spirit, when I shall be at rest. What I said to our great father in Washington I say again—I will always listen to him. I am done.'"

When he had had time to think about it, Black Hawk apparently regretted his outburst and asked that his words be "blotted out." Then, in all his dignity, he arose to express his appreciation to Keokuk for caring for his wife and children during his absence.

"I thank them for it," Black Hawk said. "The Great Spirit knows I thank them. Before the sun sets behind the hills tomorrow, I shall see them...I shall soon be far away. I shall have no village, no band. I shall live alone."

Drawing by Henry Lewis.

He left to live alone with his family near what is now Selma, Iowa, near Ottumwa, in a gentle curve of the Des Moines River. There he lived in a cabin and dressed like a white man. The few who saw him said the old spark of the warrior appeared to be gone. Nearby was the home of Black Hawk's long-time friend, the trader Jim Jordan, to whom the chief had given great tracts of land.

Word was sent to Black Hawk that the important men of the Sauk and Fox tribes were being called to Rock Island to attend a conference with government commissioners. It is probable that the invitation to Black Hawk was only a courtesy gesture because he no longer ruled the tribes. He started for the meeting, but became ill and returned home.

On Oct. 3, 1838, at the age of 71, 'Ma-'kata-wimesheka-'ka of Saukenuk' or Black Hawk, died of pneumonia. With few to mourn him, he was buried in simple services. Residents of Selma say Black Hawk was buried in a mound near the river. But even in death, he was to suffer a final indignity.

The trader Jordan related the story that three men had come in the night and removed the body from the burial mound. Jordan reportedly followed their tracks. When he returned a few days later, all he would say of the chase was a cryptic, "Two of the thieves got away."

Though historians disagree on just what happened, there is general agreement that a Dr. James Turner was somehow involved in the theft of Black Hawk's body. In his book "The Story of Iowa," historian William Petersen says Dr. Turner took the body, intending to mount it for exhibition. But he claims the indignation of both whites and Indians caused Dr. Turner to return the body.

A more grisly account is given by another historian who says details of the theft were described in 1894 by Mrs. Welch Nossaman, who was 14 years old at the time of Black Hawk's death. She was reportedly acting as a nurse to Dr. Turner's sister-in-law when he plotted the grave-robbing.

"One day I heard the doctor say that if he could only steal Black Hawk's head, he could make a fortune out of it by taking it east and putting it on ex-hibition," Mrs. Nossaman said. "We knew the evening he went to steal the head, and sat up to await his coming. He got in with it at four o'clock and hid it till the afternoon of the same day when he cooked the flesh off the skull."

Some historians believe Dr. Turner also cooked the flesh off the rest of Black Hawk's skeleton, and that he was assisted in stealing the body by two men—Warren and Jefferson Cox. They were said to have provided the container for boiling Black Hawk's bones—their mother's large iron kettle in which she made soap. About two feet in circumference and a foot deep, the kettle once hung in the Rock Island's Black Hawk State Park Museum, donated by a granddaughter of Warren Cox.

Jordan, the trader, reportedly appealed to Gov. Robert Lucas of the new Territory of Iowa, to help recover Black Hawk's remains. And at the same time, some Indians in warpaint appeared at the Turner cabin in Lexington, Van Buren County, and demanded that the doctor be turned over to them. Turner's brother, William, managed to stall the Indians, while Dr. Turner fled, taking Black Hawk's bones with him, some historians say. The doctor is said to have left the bones with another doctor named Hollowbush in Quincy, Ill.

Hollowbush apparently feared he would get into trouble with the law and turned the bones over to the mayor of Quincy. Gov. Lucas, ordered that the skeleton be taken to Burlington, Iowa, and deposited in the Geological and Historical Society building there. Black Hawk's widow and other members of his family agreed to this.

The Turner family, including the doctor, went to St. Louis, where within three years all were dead of cholera.

In 1855, fire destroyed the museum in Burlington. The bones of Black Hawk mingled with the ashes of the building and were lost forever. Finally, a proud warrior could rest in peace. □

Drawing by Henry Lewis.

A FORGOTTEN BATTLE

For years, the fact that the northernmost battle of the Revolutionary War was fought in what is now the Quad-Cities lay buried in the archives of Virginia, until it was finally brought to light by an historian. And a strange tale it is, studded with the names that are an integral part of America's history and heritage.

The story involves an unlikely assortment of men, Spanish, French and Americans, unlike, but with a common bond — undying hatred of the British. One summer day in 1770 they would perform a deed that would not even find its way into the history books, yet, in its way, was most important.

Drawing by Henry Lewis.

For this tattered, ill-equipped group did make history by taking part in the most northern extension of the Revolutionary War in the Mississippi Valley. And they did it virtually unassisted, and certainly, unsung.

During the Revolutionary War, the Sauk and Fox Indians, who inhabited the Mississippi Valley and what is now the Quad-City area, became allies of Great Britain through their friendship with the English traders. Accordingly, when war broke out between the United States and England, the Sauks left their village of Saukenuk, the birthplace of Chief Black Hawk near the mouth of the Rock River in what is now Rock Island. And the Fox warriors smeared on warpaint and left their village, called "Oskosh," and later, "Morgan," on the present site of the City of Davenport. Together, the two tribes joined the British for a planned attack on St. Louis.

When Col. George Rogers Clark learned of the plans, he rushed to the aid of Lt. Col. John Montgomery, who was commander of a small garrison of 350 men at Kahokia, Mo.

Pooling their resources, the Americans beat off the attack on St. Louis and sent the British and Indians fleeing in disorder up the Illinois and Mississippi Rivers. Clark then ordered Montgomery to pursue the enemy up the Illinois River and to strike across country to destroy the villages of the Sauk and Fox. Montgomery has been described by historians as "an Irishman full of fight." Officially, he was "commander of Virginia troops in the county of Illinois."

With Spaniards from the St. Louis area (Spain had entered the war against England in 1779), two companies from the French settlements, and the rest American soldiers, Montgomery set out in pursuit of the enemy.

He was hampered, though, by a serious lack of supplies. He noted this deficiency in a letter to Col. Clark, in which he said, "I can't tell what to do in regard of clothing for the soldiers. As the goods you sent me is gone, I would be glad that if it is in your power to send a little relefe to me for the soldiers. If it is only as much as will make them a little jump jacote and a pear of overalls I think they will scuffle threw."

Back came the reply, several weeks later, from Patrick Henry, governor of Virginia, from which the troops' command originated. Henry said that Clark and Montgomery would do well to withdraw their troops from the search for Indian villages.

With devastating abruptness, Henry stated, "You need expect no help or supplies from this state." Montgomery took the rebuff like a good soldier and continued to carry out Col. Clark's orders. He left Kahokia on June 4 with his 350 men, and marched to the lake opening on the Illinois River, and from there to the Rock River in Rock Island County, destroying the Indian villages and crops on the way.

Still stunned by the defeat at Kahokia, the Indians in most cases offered little or no resistance. There was a battle with the Sauk Indians at Saukenuk at the mouth of the Rock River, but Montgomery made little mention of it, probably never dreaming of its historical importance, though it possibly involved 700 braves, and the Sauk and Fox were known to always give a good account of themselves in a fight.

The battle was later recounted to Lt. Zebulon Pike, by James Aird, a trader who dealt with the Indians. Pike at the time headed a party exploring the Mississippi River.

Aird told Pike that after the battle, Montgomery had been victorious and had burned the Indian village. The settlement had been established about 1730 and was one of the largest Indian communities in the country. Estimates of its population ranged from 3,000 to 11,000.

It is also very possible that this northernmost battle in America's War for Independence stretched clear across the river to Davenport. This would seem to be indicated by a letter from Capt. John Rogers, who commanded one of Montgomery's companies. Capt. Rogers wrote, "We burn the towns of the Saux (Sauk) and Reynards (Fox)." If it is true that the Fox tribe shared the fate of the Sauk, it is very possible that the area was involved in this battle of the Revolutionary War. But the exact facts are lost in history, probably forever. □

HANDSHAKES AND A MASSACRE

During American's war with Great Britain in 1812, the English were putting strong pressure against the outnumbered soldiers at the U.S. fort in Prairie du Chien, Wis. The British and Americans at the time were struggling for the entire, rich Mississippi Valley, and control of the fort was a vital factor for either side.

In July, 1814, Lt. John Campbell, with a force of 120 U.S. regulars and militia in three keelboats, came up the river from St. Louis, intending to reinforce and re-supply the fort at Prairie du Chien. Lt. Campbell had no way of knowing his plans had been learned by Pierre Rolett, a French-Canadian Indian trader who served as an agent of the British. One of Rolett's duties was to keep the Sauk and Fox Indians loyal to the British. Rolett and other English or English-allied traders had, unlike the Americans, always made it a point to be scrupulously fair when dealing with the Indians. Black Hawk, chief of the Sauks and Foxes, trusted the English and readily agreed to help them.

The Campbell expedition anchored at Rock Island on its way upstream and there were received in quite friendly fashion by Black Hawk and his people, who spent two days aboard the keelboats eating and drinking with the Americans. Observing this, Rolett is said to have called Black Hawk and his council to a secret conference, informing them it was time for them to aid Great Britain.

Never suspecting treachery, Lt. Campbell and his men became friendly with the Indians. They didn't know as they passed upstream through the ever-dangerous Rock Island Rapids, that Black Hawk and 500 braves were concealed along the river, watching their every move. A few miles upstream, as it was passing a small island, Lt. Campbell's boat was blown to shore and grounded after striking a large rock.

The Indians took this opportunity to set upon their "friends" of the night before, and massacred many of them before the other boats could come to the rescue. Lt. Campbell himself was shot in the left side, shoulder and arm, an injury that left his arm useless for the rest of his life. Sixteen of Campbell's men were killed and 21 wounded. That same day, British forces overran the fort at Prairie du Chien and ran up their flag. They held the fort, and domination over the Mississippi Valley, until the end of the war.

Black Hawk and his braves plundered Lt. Campbell's boat and scalped the dead, later returning to their village opposite the lower end of Rock Island to celebrate with feasting and dancing. They also hoisted the Union Jack in what is now approximately the center of downtown Rock Island. Thereafter, the island on which the attack occurred was known as "Campbell's Island," a name it bears to this day.

There is a strange sequel to this story, though it may be only legend. It is said that years later, the steamboat General Pike was ascending the Mississippi when it ran aground at the very spot where Campbell's boat had foundered. To keep from hitting the same big rock, known as "Campbell's Rock," the General Pike anchored in the current.

A tall, moody man was standing by the rail, watching the water when someone mentioned that the person who had engineered Campbell's defeat was aboard the boat.

The man at the rail demanded to know where Rolett might be, and went immediately to the trader's cabin. When he made certain of Rolett's identity, he revealed himself to be John Campbell. Pointing to his useless arm, he accused the pale and shaken Rolett of being responsible for it.

Drawing by Henry Lewis.

He reportedly held a knife at Rolett's throat and offered him two choices — to stay and have his throat slit, or to leap upon Campbell's Rock and either drown or swim to the island. According to the story, Rolett quickly jumped, clung to the rock until he was exhausted, and finally made it to the island, only to be left behind by the boat. If the story is true, it was the only measure of revenge Lt. Campbell would ever know for a treacherous massacre. □

A FUTURE PRESIDENT LOSES A BATTLE ON THE MISSISSIPPI

Many were the destinies shaped in part by the Mississippi River. The "Father of Waters" played taciturn host to future presidents, generals, authors and explorers, and was singularly unimpressed with all of them.

A lean, tough young major in the Army of the United States didn't know on a September day in 1814 what fate held for him. He only knew that a hard job lay ahead — to sail up the Mississippi from St. Louis and destroy the villages of the Sauk and Fox Indians along the river, and, if possible, to engage and defeat their English allies.

The villages were located in what is now the area of Davenport, Iowa, and Rock Island, Illinois. The United States, through the Louisiana Purchase, had doubled its territory in 1803. But the boundaries, particularly around the mouth of the Mississippi, were uncertain.

England at the time was engaged in an all-out war with France. Some Americans cast covetous eyes at the vast territory of Canada. They were dismayed, too, that the English disputed the Americans' new boundaries and incited the Indians to fight the ever-encroaching Yankee tide.

On June 18, 1812, the Congress of the United States declared war on England, oblivious to the fact America was ill-prepared for conflict, and its troops poorly trained and equipped. The Sauk and Fox, a mighty Indian nation, had lined up with the British, primarily because English traders had made it a point to be scrupulously fair with them, something that couldn't always be said for the Americans.

The strange war in the virtually uncharted regions went on month after month with minor victories and reverses on both sides. On Sept. 5, 1814, the young major with his force of 334 soldiers sailed up the

Mississippi, not knowing Indian spies had told the enemy of their coming, and that a force of British regulars, backed by 1,500 Indians, was waiting to massacre them.

British cannon pointed their snouts toward the passages through which the Americans had to come. Heavily armed Indians hid in the bushes along the shore, ready to pounce on the Americans after the cannons had sunk the boats. The little fleet of eight, hard-to-maneuver keel boats came slowly up the river. Flying from the major's lead boat was a large white flag with which he hoped to lure the Indians to a council — and then attack them.

Indians and their villages began to appear along the river, but the troops moved past them without firing a shot. The major hoped to fool them into thinking he was en route to reinforce the American garrison at Prairie du Chien, Wis. He didn't know the fort had already fallen to the British. After destroying the Indian villages, the major intended to construct a fort in the area.

As his boats passed the mouth of the Rock River in Illinois, the wind shifted suddenly and increased in velocity. It had reached gale proportions by the time the Americans reached the western tip of a piece of land called Credit Island, now a part of the City of Davenport, Iowa. It was impossible for them to go on, though they knew there were Indians on the island and all around them. They were forced to put in at a small body of land called Pelican Island, near the larger island.

All night the sodden soldiers huddled in the howling rain. Just as day was breaking, Indians waded across the river, crept onto the smaller island, and murdered an American corporal posted as a guard. The major rallied his forces and tried to pursue the Indians through the heavy brush, but when he reached the opposite side of Pelican Island, he found the Indians had waded back to the larger Credit Island.

The American troops began firing across the narrow stretch of water with their small cannons. The Indians replied with volleys of musket fire that badly wounded two soldiers. As the Americans took to their boats and headed downstream in an attempt to destroy a collection of Indian canoes, the hidden British troops cut loose from behind a knoll with their six-pounders and swivel guns. One American boat was instantly shattered by direct hits and others were damaged.

The Americans tried to fire back, but in the swirling water their shots went wild. They fled downstream under a constant artillery barrage. Indians on the shore harassed them with small arms fire. Eventually, the battered Americans eluded their pursuers and landed downstream on the Illinois shore. Many soldiers were dead or wounded, and the boats were badly damaged or had sunk. Surveying the situation, and knowing he was out-numbered and out-gunned, the major decided to abandon the mission and headed back downstream to St. Louis.

For this action he was reproached by his superiors and his military career seemed in jeopardy. Shortly after this expedition, the Treaty of Ghent was signed and on Dec. 24, 1814, the War of 1812 officially ended.

The major left the Army because his rank had been lowered due to a reduction to peace time strength. This, though, was not the end but the beginning of his service. In 1816, he was reappointed to his old rank, and followed 20 years of garrison life. Later he would fight in the same area of his defeat against the wily war chief of the Sauks and Foxes, Black Hawk. Still later, he would be known as the hero of war with Mexico, would hold the rank of general, and would proudly bear the nickname of "Old Rough and Ready."

But more than any of these things, Zachary Taylor would always be remembered as the twelfth President of the United States. □

◀

Zachary Taylor from the University of Iowa Presidential Collection and Display of the University of Iowa Library.

Two bolts of calico were the fare for one of the first ferry crossings of the Mississippi River, though the boat made its round-trip maiden voyage with neither passengers nor cargo.

Capt. Benjamin W. Clark, a big, gruff man who spoke no more than was necessary, just puffed on his pipe and kept sawing and hammering when others declared he was crazy to think he could cross the Mississippi from Andalusia, Ill., to Buffalo, Iowa, with a boat big enough to carry passengers and cargo. The river was too swift and the currents

Early drawing of ferry. (Buffalo Bill Museum Collection.)

too treacherous, the scoffers said. They predicted Capt. Clark not only would lose his boat, but would probably be drowned, too.

In the early 1800's a ferry between the Iowa and Illinois shores was badly needed, and Capt. Clark was a daring and imaginative man who was certain he could provide it. Earlier, he had established the town of Buffalo, and is believed to have been the first Scott County settler, though he still lived in Andalusia when he built his ferry.

A company of French traders camped on the river bank near Buffalo one night and learned from the settlers that Capt. Clark had finally completed his boat. They guffawed loudly at the news, declaring

Circa 1900 ferry. (Buffalo Bill Museum Collection.)

that only "Ze crazy Americans" would be foolish enough to believe they could cross the river with such a large craft.

The more they thought about it the funnier it seemed and finally, fortified by liquid refreshments, they congregated upon the river bank, calling loudly for Capt. Clark to send the ferry across. Trying to keep from laughing, they declared they had a drove of cattle to be ferried across.

Capt. Clark knew that in those early days there were no herds of cattle about, but they had ordered his ferry, and his ferry they would get. He was known as a stern, uncompromising man, but those who knew him well suspected there was a sense of humor under that gruff exterior.

He ordered his men to get the boat ready and set out quietly for the Iowa shore while the taunts of the Frenchmen were still echoing across the river. It was quite dark and the Frenchmen couldn't see the big boat, propelled by oars, approaching with stern-visaged Capt. Clark standing at the helm and steering over the swelling waves.

The boat was almost to their campsite when the traders spotted it. Then they all laughed and rolled on the ground and said what fools the Americans were because it was all a joke and they had nothing to be ferried across the river.

The captain's face was beet red, a warning signal to those who knew him, and without a word he stalked into the traders' camp, stared them down, and demanded $10 as his fee for ferriage.

Suddenly the joke didn't seem so funny to the Frenchmen. Capt. Clark stood before them, arms folded, his face like granite. Behind him stood his stalwart crewmen. After a quick consultation, the traders reluctantly agreed the captain should be paid for his trip. The only problem was they didn't have $10 among them.

Then one trader had an inspiration. "Would the good captain perhaps accept two bolts of calico?" In those early days this was considered good legal tender, especially among the Indians. Capt. Clark waited long enough to worry the traders a bit, and then nodded his agreement.

There was no more laughter from the Frenchmen's camp as Capt. Clark and his crew returned to their boat and paddled away in the darkness.

Capt. Clark's ferry not only proved to be quite feasible and profitable, but for many years was the only place between Burlington and Dubuque where one could cross the Mississippi with cargo. □

Drawing by Henry Lewis.

THEY NAMED A RIVER

To some, the name "Wapsipinicon" is too much of a tongue-twister, and they prefer to refer simply to the little river that twists its way through much of Iowa to the Mississippi, as "The Wapsi."

This shortening, while admittedly easier, leaves out one of the very important characters that, according to one legend, gave the winding river its unusual name. A grand and romantic legend it is, too. Is it the truth? Who can say?

It involves a lovely Indian princess named Wapsi, a brave warrior who lover her, and a jealous suitor

◀

Drawing by Henry Lewis.

who vowed she would belong to no one but himself. The maiden, Wapsi, was known for her grace and beauty and was the favorite daughter of the Sauk chief, Good Heart. Legend says that after her mother's death, her father lavished all his love upon her. To her were given the lightest canoes, the brightest beads, the softest skins. But unspoiled by such pampering, she remained gentle and generous, and much sought after by the braves of her tribe.

For a long time the Indians in eastern Iowa had been at peace, but this tranquility was shattered one day when a Sauk brave was found dead, his body studded with arrows fired by the bloodthirsty Crows.

Chief Good Heart immediately called a war council, and far into the night the drums spoke of war and vengeance. The Sauk asked the fierce Sioux to help punish the enemy. One of the Sioux warriors who responded to the plea for assistance was Pinicon, stalwart young son of Chief Black Feather.

The son of Black Feather and the daughter of Good Heart met, according to the legend, and soon had eyes for none other. The braves of the Sauk and Sioux hunted down the Crows and collected many scalps. And then there was time for Wapsi and Pinicon to walk together in the woods and to declare their love for one another. In time they announced plans to wed.

Chief Good Heart, Wapsi's father, was delighted and accepted the Sioux warrior as his own son. Though disappointed, her many other suitors in the Sauk tribe wished her well, that is, all but one. Fleet Foot had long coveted Wapsi and he hated the Sioux brave who had thwarted his plans to wed her. He vowed that Pinicon should never have her.

Drawing by Henry Lewis.

On their wedding night, Wapsi and Pinicon drifted languidly down a small stream in their canoe, too absorbed with one another to notice that Fleet Foot had followed them and was watching from the river banks. As Pinicon leaned forward to whisper to his new bride, he lightly touched her fingers to his lips. Fleet Foot saw the gesture and angrily fitted an arrow into his bow. He took careful aim and the shaft buried itself in Pinicon's chest.

With a cry of alarm, Wapsi sprang toward her mortally wounded lover. As she did so, the canoe overturned, and, clasped in one another's arms, the two sank beneath the rushing waters.

And they say today, if you stand on the banks of the Wapsipinicon, and are very quiet, you can still hear in the ripples the drowned lovers talking to one another. Fact or legend? No one can say. □

■

A WILD AND WACKY VOYAGE

There has probably, for sheer improbability, never been another trip quite like that of the "Virginia," the first steamboat to attempt the perilous journey from St. Louis, up the uncharted Mississippi River to the Falls of St. Anthony, now known as Minneapolis.

No captain had ever been foolhardy enough to attempt such an expedition, for the year was 1823, and the lands through which any boat would have to pass were marked on maps only as "Savage Country," unsettled except for scattered dots of civilization such as Fort Armstrong, on what is now Arsenal Island. This was the land dominated by the Indian, by wily Indian leaders such as Black Hawk, and everyone was certain it was sheer insanity to venture into it aboard a steamboat.

The scoffers predicted the Virginia would be shattered on rocks, or sink, or explode straining against the vicious currents. The passengers would either drown or be slain by Indians. To make the voyage even more absurd, the Virginia's crew was ill-trained, and the passenger roster wouldn't have been believable even in a Hollywood script.

There was, for example, Major Lawrence Taliaferro, an Indian agent at Fort Anthony; Giacomo Constantine Beltrami, an Italian exile and romanticist who told the startled Indians he had come from the moon; a Sauk chief and his two naked children; a Kentucky family, whose baggage included crated

chickens, a goat, cats and dogs; and a woman missionary described by Beltrami as "one of those good women who devoted themselves to God only when they have lost all hope of pleasing men."

The records of this strange journey were kept by Beltrami, cavalier, wit and prodigious consumer of whiskey. He made two records of his diary, one of which went to a countess in Italy, while the other was later published. In the spring of 1823, the Virginia swung out into the channel at St. Louis and headed confidently upstream. Beltrami described the boat as "a miserable 2,000 tons of burden."

The first few days were uneventful. During that time, Beltrami became friends with the Indian Chief Great Eagle, who confided that the Virginia's pilot was a fool and not to be trusted, advice the Italian would later find to be quite true. When the Virginia stopped at the site of what is now Quincy, Ill., Beltrami went ashore, following a flock of wild turkeys.

"Suddenly I was lost, and when I found my way back to the river, the Virginia was gone," he wrote. Cursing the pilot, Beltrami stumbled through heavy brush along the river, and finally spotted the unimpressive sternwheeler stranded on a sandbar. A canoe was dispatched to take him aboard. At this moment, the surprised Beltrami saw three figures leap off the boat and into the river. Great Eagle, disgusted that the pilot had ignored his warnings about the channel, had abandoned ship with his two children. But the next day when the boat arrived at Fort Edward, there was Great Eagle on hand to meet it with his people. The chief had come to retrieve some things he'd left aboard ship. He greeted

Drawing by Henry Lewis.

Rounding a bend in the river, the Virginia was suddenly confronted in the distance with, in Beltrami's words, "an exquisitely blended view of Fort Armstrong." The fort stood on a rocky plateau, at what is now the Rock Island Arsenal approach to the Government Bridge.

Happy to see anyone from the "outside world," jubilant soldiers at the fort fired four resounding cannon salutes, while men along the shore discharged muskets into the air. The crew rested for a few days before attempting to navigate the very treacherous Rock Island Rapids. Beltrami took advantage of the delay to visit Saukenuk, largest village of the Sauk tribe, on the banks of the Rock River.

The Indians were mystified by this man who was neither French, English, Spanish or American. One evening as he sat with the Sauks around the fire, Beltrami confided that he had come from the moon. The Indians were so impressed they treated him with reverence and gave him choice foods.

There were many adventures and close calls on the trip to the Falls of St. Anthony, but the strange assortment of people finally completed it and claimed the honor of having been the first steamboat passengers to navigate the wild river through the untamed land. □

Beltrami warmly and gave him the scalp of a Sioux which he wore on the handle of his tomahawk.

Now the Virginia entered into treacherous, rapid-strewn water. At what is now Keokuk, Iowa, she foundered through the "Rapids of the Moine," got hung up on a ledge, and was two days getting started again.

Beltrami was fascinated by the scenes of beauty that unfolded along the Mississippi as the Virginia chugged upriver. Alarmed Indians, thinking the boat a fire-breathing monster, watched its progress in horror from behind trees. A band of Fox Indians was watching the boat below what is now Muscatine one night when it blew off steam, and sent them scurrying in fear into the woods.

Early steamboats on the river.

END OF THE WORLD

Fort Armstrong, which later became the Rock Island Arsenal, the largest defense unit of its kind in the world, played a key role in the development of the wilderness area that today is the home of more than 350,000 people. The Rock Island Arsenal still is vital to the economy of the area and the defense of the nation.

It had a stormy, 20-year career as Fort Armstrong, and was often considered "the end of the world" by soldiers assigned there. Duty at the post, isolated in the middle of the Mississippi River, was often so boring that, as one historian says, "one of the calisthentics of the service in those days was deserting."

Three defeats by Indians after the end of the War of 1812, and a determination to insure the free passage of lead barges from Dubuque and Galena to St. Louis, led the U.S. government to construct Fort Armstrong in 1816.

Gen. Thomas Smith and Major William Lawrence and their men converged on the island and chose its western extremity as the site for a fort. When the Indians refused to meet with Gen. Smith, he took his men on to Ft. Shelby, leaving Lawrence to construct the fort. Lawrence proceeded to do this with the 800 soldiers of the 8th Infantry.

In 1819, the fort was described as "300 feet square, with three block houses mounting three six-pounders. The barracks are of sufficient size to accommodate three companies. The magazine is of stone. The commanding officer's quarters consists of a center two-story building 28 feet in length and a piazza built in front and rear."

Col. George Davenport, for whom the City of Davenport was named, was the fort's sutler, or storekeeper. He loaded several boats with provisions in St. Louis and sent a herd of cattle overland to feed the soldiers. Davenport's home on the island was a double log cabin which also served as an Indian trading post. In 1817, Davenport gave up his sutler's post, but continued to maintain his home on the island until years later when he was slain by bandits. The restored home may be seen there today.

The fort was completed in 1817, so formidable and well-manned that the Sauk and Fox Indians who inhabited the area didn't dare attack it. The years passed quietly and soldiers stationed at Fort Armstrong found time hanging very heavily on their hands. To keep busy, they lobbed cannonballs across the river at the Iowa embankment that is now East Sixth and Seventh Streets at LeClaire and Farnam Streets in Davenport. They worked in a garden planted south and east of the fort. They consumed as much liquor as seven dollars a month could buy. They dallied with Indian squaws when the occasion presented itself. And they deserted in fairly large numbers.

The first white settlers, bringing a measure of civilization with them, didn't start to arrive in the area until about 1828, and anything that would make life a little more tolerable for bored soldiers just didn't exist. The fort was shaken out of its torpor in 1831, though, when Chief Black Hawk and his tribes, driven from their Illinois villages by government decree, crossed the river from Iowa and attempted to reclaim their lands. The governor of Illinois sent the state militia to join the Fort Armstrong troops to punish the Indians. The soldiers and volunteers took part in a bloodless battle, burning a deserted Indian village, but this was only a prelude to the bloody Black Hawk War, which broke out the following year.

In 1832, Gen. Atkinson was ordered to Ft. Armstrong. As they chased Black Hawk up the Rock River, the troops behaved as if they were on a picnic. The volunteers abandoned a trail of equipment, fought among themselves, murdered one of Black Hawk's emissaries under a flag of truce, and generally acted so outrageously that a mass discharge was the only answer.

Some say the treaty ending the Black Hawk War was signed at Fort Armstrong, others that it was signed at the site of the home of Antoine LeClaire, founder of the City of Davenport. After the short-lived Black Hawk War, Fort Armstrong lapsed once more into its lethargy, though it always served as a strong deterrent against Indian uprisings. The old fort was shut down in 1836, the year the City of

Davenport was platted. In 1840, the fort was converted to an ordnance depot, but in 1845 it was abandoned and allowed to fall into partial ruin. The Army quartermaster sold some of the lumber, and in 1855, fire swept the buildings. The charred remains were torn down in 1863, and some of the wood was used in construction of the first Rock Island Arsenal building. Today all that remains of Fort Armstrong are two big blocks of wood in the Arsenal's John M. Browning Museum. □

Drawing by Henry Lewis.

Drawing by Henry Lewis.

LEGEND OF THE LOVERS

Among the many legacies left by the Indians who once inhabited what is now the Quad-City area are legends, some happy, some sad, but all colorful and quite fanciful. The Indians loved these stories and many of them have become part of our folklore, too.

One of these was told by Chief Black Hawk, great leader of the Sauk and Fox, who made their homes in the areas which are now Davenport and Rock Island. Black Hawk related that in 1827 a young Sioux Indian brave became lost in a snowstorm and eventually found his way into a Sauk village.

The Sauk and Sioux were blood enemies, but Indian custom demanded the unwelcome visitor be afforded every measure of safety and hospitality under the circumstances. The young brave remained with the Sauks for some time while the storm howled around their village. While the brave was there, he fell in love with the daughter of one of the Sauk warriors, Black Hawk said.

The Sioux brave knew full well the Sauk would never consent to their marriage, but he vowed he would return sometime in the summer and take the girl away with him. The following July, Black Hawk recounted, the brave rode up to the Rock River village of the Sauks and hid himself in the woods.

When he saw his sweetheart hoeing corn in the field with her mother, he waited until late afternoon when the older woman returned to the village. Then he gave a long, low whistle, their pre-arranged signal of his return. Unhurriedly, the girl hoed to the end of the row. When she reached it, she ran with pounding heart to greet her lover. She promised to leave with him for his tribe as soon as she could return to her lodge to get her blanket.

What the lovers didn't know, Black Hawk related, was that their meeting has been observed by the girl's two brothers. Grabbing their guns, the brothers followed the pair, intending to slay the hated Sioux. But the lovers realized they were being followed and started to run. And as they ran, a sudden storm developed and it began to rain very hard.

The lovers hastened to a kind of semi-cave under the rocks at the very bottom of the watch tower in what is now Black Hawk State Park in Rock Island. There, for a time at least, they felt they were safe from the storm and the angry brothers.

But as they embraced, there was a sudden flash of lightning, followed by a terrible rumble of thunder. The rock cliff above them shattered and fell, burying the lovers forever under tons of rock. There, according to the legend, the lovers still remain in their final embrace.

Some say if you stand very quietly at the base of the cliff under Black Hawk's watch tower today, and listen very closely, you can sometimes hear a sound like low sobbing. Scoffers will tell you it is only the wind blowing off Rock River.

This was the tale told by Black Hawk, and he had the reputation of being an honest man.

CHIEF'S REVENGE

A Sauk and Fox war chief, painted by George Catlin.

A broken promise, deceit, bloodshed and swift revenge combined to give what is now the City of Davenport its first name — "Morgan," — in honor of a half-breed Indian chief who repaid treachery with death.

Blood enemies of the Sauk and Fox tribes who inhabited the Mississippi River Valley were the fierce Sioux, Chippewas, Winnebagoes and Memomenies. Whenever the chance presented itself, they mercilessly ambushed one another.

The continual warfare, though, had seriously reduced the ranks of the Sauks and Foxes so they readily agreed in the spring of 1828 when the Sioux and their allies, through the Indian agent at Prairie du Chien, sent them an invitation for a meeting to draw up a truce.

More than ready for peace, the Sauk and Fox Chief, Piea-Moskie, and all his principal chiefs and braves, left their villages for the treaty meeting at Prairie du Chien. The Sauk and Foxes had no idea they were being lured into a death trap. The Winnebagoes and Sioux had deceived their agent. They planned to ambush the unsuspecting Sauk and Fox warriors and kill them.

Spies kept constant watch upon the Sauk and Foxes as they moved up river. On the second night after leaving Dubuque, the Sauks and Foxes camped just below the mouth of the Wisconsin River.

They were dozing around their campfires when more than 100 whooping members of the war party fired upon them.

It was a massacre, from which only two of the Sauk and Fox braves escaped by jumping into the river. These returned to their villages to tell of the enemy's treachery. It was a terrible blow for the Sauk and Fox tribes. Most of their leaders were dead, and many of their warriors slain, too. The survivors held a council and named as their chief a daring, half-breed known as "Morgan." He was thereupon renamed Maque-pra-um.

Quickly Morgan formed his best men into a war party to deal with the hated Sioux. Around the council fires, the braves wailed and lamented their dead. Then, in fighting garb, they screamed for blood and revenge. With blackened faces and chanting the death song, the braves leaped into their canoes and set out to avenge their brothers.

Moving silently and undetected, they arrived near Prairie du Chien and sent out spies who reported the foe was encamped almost under the guns of Fort Crawford. Chief Morgan held his war party in ambush position until dark, leaving a guard party with the canoes.

Then the warriors stripped for battle, wearing only the girdle containing the tomahawk and scalping knife. They swam the Mississippi and stealthily approached the unguarded Sioux encampment. It was dark and silent. In the first wigwam they found an Indian calmly smoking his pipe. He was quickly dragged outside and killed.

No one awakened as the Sauk and Fox warriors crept from tent to tent, their knives and tomahawks flashing in the moonlight. Only when the avenging was done, and many chiefs and braves lay dead, did the victorious Sauk and Foxes give loud whoops of

Drawing by Henry Lewis.

satisfaction and revenge that awakened sleeping soldiers in the fort. But the victors were soon across the river and heading for home in their canoes.

Early settlers recalled that the Sauk and Fox braves made a terrible sight as they came downriver, their canoes lashed side by side, and the heads and scalps of their enemies sticking from prominently-displayed poles.

Returning triumphantly to their village, the Indians displayed the trophies of the kills as they danced the "scalp dance." After much celebrating, they deserted their village at Dubuque and headed downriver.

Once again they celebrated their victory with dancing and savage cries, and as long as they lived in what is now Davenport, they called it "Morgan," in honor of the chief who had avenged a terrible wrong. □

'TAKE COMMAND, CAPT. LINCOLN!'

Representation of Abraham Lincoln as a captain in the Black Hawk War. (Augustana College Collection.)

True, the uniform hung rather scare-crow-like on his gangling frame, and the cuffs lacked several inches of reaching his wrists, but the face of the man registered intense pride and patriotism as he stood in a Rock Island County field and took the oath of allegiance that made him a soldier in the volunteer militia.

The ceremony was brief, and at its conclusion, the officer who had administered the oath saluted and snapped, "And now take over your command, Capt. Lincoln!"

One of the privates, drawn up in ranks to witness the swearing in ceremony, nudged another and rolled his eyes as he drawled, "Abe Lincoln a captain! Who'd ever have thought it?"

Lincoln later was to recall that brief moment as the proudest occasion of his life. The induction ceremony occurred approximately at the junction of the Andalusia and Ridgewood Roads in Rock Island County. The site in later years was marked by several walnut trees taken from the battlefield at Gettysburg. Lincoln was 23 years old at the time he was inducted, and thus began his first service to the nation.

Lincoln joined a group of about 2,000 men, mostly volunteers, and very few of them professional soldiers. On very short notice they had left their homes and farms to participate in the war against Black Hawk, the Sauk and Fox war chief who was burning and pillaging his former villages in western Illinois.

Straggling in unmilitary formation, the volunteers had marched 50 miles to the Rock Island County camp where they remained for a couple of days, learning some of the bare rudiments of soldiering. It was at this camp that Lincoln created one of the many legends that marked his career. Lean and immensely strong from years of hard work, Lincoln had won considerable renown as a wrestler. In no time, a group of young soldiers had promoted a wrestling match between Lincoln and an equally famed wrestler from Union County, named Dow Thompson.

Lincoln's Sangamon County boys scoffed at the idea anyone could defeat their Abe, while the Union County soldiers were willing to bet their money on their champion. Money was put up and the crowd stepped back to give the wrestlers room.

The two men seemed quite evenly matched and neither gained an advantage until Thompson, with a sudden quick movement threw Lincoln and gained the first fall. It was the first time Lincoln had ever been thrown in his life, and he marveled, "This is the strongest man I've ever met."

They went at each other again—and again Lincoln was thrown. Lincoln's backers, however, cried "foul" and a fight seemed imminent. But then, smiling, Lincoln held up his hand and declared, "Boys, give up your bets. If he hasn't thrown me fairly, he could."

The army of volunteers marched away from Rock Island County on May 10, and traveled 40 miles to Prophetstown where they expected to encounter hostile Indians. But not an Indian was to be seen in the normally bustling village, named for the "Prophet", one of Black Hawk's trusted lieutenants.

The volunteers were disgusted at the lack of action and after a few days most of them turned in their gear and went home. Lincoln, however, gave up his commission and reenlisted as a private. When that company was mustered out after a month of inactivity, he enlisted once more, this time in a company of scouts. The man who one day would be President of the United States arrived at Kellogg's Grove just after a frenzied battle with the Indians and helped bury five soldiers who had been slain there. Many years later, Lincoln recalled that gory scene.

"I remember just how those men looked as we rode up the hill where their camp had been. The red light of the morning sun was streaming upon them as they lay, heads toward us, on the ground. Every man had a round red spot on the top of his head about as big as a dollar where the Indians had taken off his scalp. It was frightful, and grotesque."

Lincoln was mustered out two months after the swearing-in in Rock Island County. Though he'd traveled hundreds of miles, he had never been involved in any action against the Indians.

Years later, Lincoln made a speech in Congress in which he recalled an anecdote of his brief sojourn in the military as an officer. He said he was drilling his company when he wished to move them through a gate.

"I could not for the life of me remember the proper word of command for getting my company endwise," he said. "So as we came near the gate, I shouted, "This company is dismissed for two minutes, when it will fall in again on the other side of the gate." □

Said to be a photo of the second campsite area where Lincoln and other soldiers of the Black Hawk War camped. (Augustana College Collection.)

IOWA'S FIRST SURGERY?

You probably could peruse the oldest medical journals and never even find a mention of what possibly was the first "surgery" ever performed in Iowa. For that matter, it's unlikely you'd find the names of John (Old Shoot) Shook, or Smith Mounts, either. And, considering the type of "operation" it was, and the tools used, perhaps it's just as well.

It took place in an isolated log cabin along the Mississippi River in Buffalo, Iowa in 1833, in the biting cold while the wind howled and piled the snow hip deep at the door.

"Old Shoot" was a woodsman, wild and untamed as the wolves that often howled around his cabin at night. He was as wise in the ways of the woods and streams as the Indians, who gave the strange white man a wide berth.

Where "Old Shoot" had come from was anyone's guess. He's attached himself to Capt. Benjamin W. Clark, Scott County's first white settler and the man who'd made the first claims in the newly-acquired Black Hawk Purchase west of the Mississippi.

Because "Old Shoot" knew well the wild areas along the Wapsipinicon River, Capt. Clark prevailed upon him to stake a claim near what is now Buena

Vista in Clinton County. "Old Shoot" built the first log house in Olive Township and established the first Buena Vista ferryboat, even if it was only an Indian canoe capable of taking two men across the river at a time.

He was a blood-chilling sight, even in a land used to strange garb and unkempt appearances. He wore a hat made of the inverted lower bill of a pelican. The Indians were certain he was one of the evil spirits who lived in caves along the river.

One winter day the temperature dropped far below zero and an icy wind stirred the snow into high drifts. "Old Shoot" had planned to hike to Buffalo for supplies that day, and he had several unkind things to say about the weather. But, dag-nab it, he'd go anyway, even if it were many, many miles away.

He pulled on his rawhide boots and struggled into several layers of the animal skin that served as his clothing. Putting his long-barreled rifle over his shoulder, he strode away, muttering, into the storm.

It was rough going for the grizzled old woodsman. Yet he covered mile after mile, the snow freezing on his face and the cold stabbing into his very bones. He was still many miles from his destination when his feet got so numb he could no longer feel them, but he stumbled on and on.

"Old Shoot" was near collapse when he finally slumped against Capt. Clark's cabin door in Buffalo, calling weakly before he lost consciousness that his feet were frozen.

The woodsman was in terrible pain, though after a few days the swelling subsided. But it was obvious something would have to be done about the toes on his right foot. The damaged flesh sloughed off, leaving the bare bones exposed. Gangrene was almost certain to occur.

As tenderly as possible, Capt. Clark, known as a gruff, humorless man, explained the situation to "Old Shoot." The toes would have to come off, he said, or the woodsman would die. The old man lis-

tened gravely and then shook his head in assent.

"Give me your bottle and leave me alone for awhile," he asked. A few minutes later he called out, "I'm ready. Bring your man."

Up to "Old Shoot's" bedside walked Smith Mounts, one of the captain's assistants. In his hands he carried a wooden mallet and a sharp, carpenter's chisel.

"Put your foot on the floor, 'Shoot,'" he ordered, "and better look the other way. This ain't going to be pleasant."

There wasn't a sound as Mounts put the chisel in place and raised the heavy wallet. Five times the mallet crashed down on the chisel with a sickening "thunk!"

"Old Shoot" paled under his full beard and gripped the bedpost until his knuckles showed white, but uttered not a sound while the "operation" was in progress. Then Mounts rose, the mallet and chisel in his hands, and looked expectantly at his "patient."

Grinning wryly, the old woodsman gave his foot an experimental twitch, winked at Capt. Clark, and growled, "You do good work, sonny. Whopped 'em off clean as a whistle, you did."

It was just a few days later, limping but ready as ever to show this wilderness who was boss, that "Old Shoot," loaded down with supplies, took the trail for home. □

HE MARRIED 'MINNEHAHA'

The husband of the Indian woman whom Henry Wadsworth Longfellow called "Minnehaha" in his famous poem "Song of Hiawatha," is buried on Rock Island Arsenal at a spot passed daily by hundreds of motorists unaware of the strange story.

A massive boulder headstone hides a century-and-a-half-old story of a white doctor's love and betrayal of a beautiful Indian maiden later immortalized in Longfellow's poem. The doctor was Dr. John Gale, an Englishman who had come to America in search of adventure. He later contracted to serve as physician with the 6th Infantry.

Few knew of Dr. Gale's marriage to the Indian maiden, Nicomi, his love for the children she bore him, and of his impossible struggle to merge the two worlds of the savage and civilized man. Nicomi had been born about 1808, of Omaha and Iowa Indian descent, near the trading post of the American Fur Co. at Bellevue. According to one story, Dr. Gale married Nicomi after she saved his life by guiding him to shelter through a blizzard.

The two lived in a comfortable log cabin near Fort Atkinson where the 6th Infantry was quartered. They were apparently quite happy. The doctor treated Nicomi tenderly and was devoted to their two children, and especially to Mary, their first-born. In 1827, the order came to abandon Fort Atkinson. The troops were ordered to move to another post downriver.

The move meant Dr. Gale would once more be living in a civilized society instead of a frontier outpost. He had enjoyed his life with his Indian wife, but balked at the idea of taking her into a world completely alien to her. There are also indications he was a bit ashamed to have his colleagues know he had married an Indian. He was so fond of his daughter, Mary, though, that he was determined to take her with him. He was certain, however, that Nicomi would never let him take the child and leave her behind, so told her nothing of his upcoming departure.

Instead, he discussed his plans with Peter Sarpy, operator of a trading post. Nicomi's brother, however, was just outside the door and overheard the doctor's plans for stealing the child. Nicomi fled with the children and hid in a cave known only to the Indians. Dr. Gale searched in vain for them, and finally departed, leaving a sum of money with Sarpy and asking him to care for his family.

As the years passed, Dr. Gale brooded about the fate of his daughter, Mary, then about nine years old. He returned to the territory around old Fort Atkinson, determined once again to find Mary and take her with him to St. Louis. In Bellevue, Iowa, the doctor learned that his other child had died. Showing more compassion than he formerly had, he made no attempt to take Mary from her mother.

In 1834, three years later, Dr. Gale returned once more to Bellevue. He was mortally ill and knew he had only a short time to live, but he felt he could die easier if he placed his daughter with a white family to be raised and educated as a white woman. But Nicomi learned of his plans and hid again in the woods until he departed.

A stone marking the grave of Dr. John Gale, with the recreated Fort Armstrong in the background. The stone and replica are near the main entrance to the present Rock Island Arsenal.

A few months later, Dr. Gale died and was buried at Fort Armstrong, now the site of Rock Island Arsenal. Following Indian custom, Nicomi observed a four-year period of mourning before marrying Sarpy, the trading post operator. In 1839, he took her to live with him in St. Louis. There they resided in a fine home, but Nicomi was miserable away from her own surroundings. Finally Sarpy allowed her to return to her wilderness home for good. He continued to be a devoted husband to his death, and provided generously for Nicomi and Mary in his will.

Nicomi lived to be quite old, and was admired by her Indian friends and respected by whites. She died in 1888. During the first half of the 19th century, the accounts of her courtship by Dr. Gale were widely circulated. Her Indian name means "Voice of the Waters." It is said Longfellow heard of Nicomi's strange story and the poem "Song of Hiawatha" was suggested in part by it, with Minnehaha (Laughing Water) representing Nicomi.

In 1962, the remains of Dr. Gale and of Dr. Richard M. Coleman, an assistant surgeon who had been buried next to him, were disinterred from a spot on the Arsenal Island marked by two boulders, and reburied with military rites in the shadow of the replica of Fort Armstrong on the Arsenal's Fort Armstrong Avenue.

The two large boulders were placed on the transferred graves and still serve as headstones. But the factual marker on Dr. Gale's grave gives no inkling of the stranger-than-fiction life he led. □

THAT STRANGE ELECTION

For unadulterated wackiness and sheer chicanery, there has probably never been anything to surpass the no-holds-barred battle between Davenport and Rockingham to decide which should be the county seat of Scott County.

There was skulduggery and scheming and intricate plotting on both sides, mixed with an earthy pioneer sense of humor that could consider the whole affair a massive practical joke — after it was finally over.

At that time, the village of Rockingham was located opposite the mouth of the Rock River in what is now west Davenport. A separate community, founded in 1835, a year earlier than Davenport, Rockingham also surpassed Davenport in size and population.

Being the county seat gave any town eminence, and both Davenport and Rockingham were determined to have that honor. Residents of both settlements had first decided to let the issue be resolved by the legislature of the Territory of Wisconsin, of which Scott County was then a part. But when evidence of bribery and conniving among that body was disclosed, it was decided to put the matter to a vote of the inhabitants.

There was little doubt then that Rockingham would win the election because it could naturally be expected to poll the most votes. That is, if the election were fairly conducted. And that was a very big "if." Election returns were to be made to Gov. Dodge of Wisconsin.

If Davenport didn't have enough legal votes, it had several influential citizens who knew how and where to get votes of another type. They met and entered into a contract with a man named Bellows, from Dubuque.

Bellows agreed, for board, whiskey, lodging and a certain sum of cash, to provide Davenport "voters" at so much a head. Into Davenport on election day came what later was called the "Bellows Express," 11 sleighloads containing the rum-soaked dregs of the Dubuque and Snake Diggings lead mines.

An early historian described these imported voters as "the most wretched looking rowdies and vagabonds that ever appeared on the streets of Davenport. They were filled with impudence, soaked in whiskey, and done up in rags," he said. From across the river in Illinois came similar "voters," ready to declare themselves staunch citizens of Davenport. No one at the polls questioned them, however.

It was a quite different story in Rockingham. Certain of victory, residents there observed a strict, honest and impartial method of voting. Imagine their astonishment, then, when Davenport racked up far more votes, enough to give it the county seat by an easy margin!

Back to Dubuque rolled the "Bellows Express," its ruffian voters having consumed 10 barrels of whiskey, in addition to costing Davenporters more than $3,000 in cash. There was great rejoicing in Davenport, but it was short-lived. A Rockingham delegation provided Gov. Dodge with documents proving fraud and trickery on the part of Davenport. The governor refused to issue his certificate of election. The next legislature passed an act calling for another election.

Wiser this time, Rockingham residents vowed to cast scruples aside and fight the sneaky Davenporters on their own terms. The campaign got under way with a vengeance. The entire county was canvassed and every available voter pledged to one side or the other. A Rockingham mill operator, "quite by chance," happened to hire a large number of extra "outside" hands around election day. On that day, ballot boxes were stuffed, while numerous "non-residents" blithely swore they were "old settlers." Poll books bore names no one had ever heard of.

Though a committee from Davenport had been sent to Rockingham to keep watch at the polls, they found when the ballot boxes were emptied there were far many more votes cast than there were citizens. The returns were made to the sheriff of Dubuque County, and this time, Rockingham was found to have the most votes.

That is, it had the most votes until the sheriff's commissioners, for some reason, took it upon themselves to "purge the polls," throwing out enough votes to make Davenport the winner. It was then declared the county seat.

Irate Rockingham residents applied to the Supreme Court for a mandamus directing the commissioners of Dubuque County to declare Rockingham the winner. The court eventually decided it had no jurisdiction in the matter, but gave an opinion that Rockingham should be the county seat. When the legislature met again, it passed an act for a third election.

Two other settlements by this time aspired to be named the county seat. One was an area called the "Geographical Center," (later Sloperville), while the other was a quarter section of land at the mouth of Duck Creek, called "Winfield," or "the Duck Creek Cornfield." The "Geographical Center," however, withdrew as a contender before the election.

Eventually, Rockingham and Davenport began offering town lots and money for county use if they should be named the county seat. Residents of both areas pledged thousands of dollars and large areas of land, and gave bonds to secure it to the county.

Eventually, Rockingham residents agreed to withdraw if Davenport would, free of expense to the county, build a courthouse and jail. The offer was accepted and Davenport easily outdistanced little Winfield to win the election.

Thus ended amicably one of the strangest election hassles in Scott County's history. Leading opponents from both sides met at a peace parley at the Rockingham Hotel in 1840, and buried the hatchet at a grand ball that lasted all night. □

A BISHOP AND A PRINCE

Drawing by Henry Lewis.

Stephenson (later Rock Island)." The next night he noted that he preached in "the village of Davenport," then a part of the Wisconsin Territory.

When the bishop crossed the river to Rock Island, he found there an invitation to preach the next night in Rockingham, which adjoined Davenport and is now a part of the city.

"Crossed over the third time the river justly called the 'Father of Waters,'" he wrote, "rode down its banks to Rockingham, that rapidly growing place to which I had been so kindly invited, where I preached in the afternoon."

After he left, the bishop wrote of his experiences, "In reflecting on these three villages — Stephenson, Davenport and Rockingham — my mind is deeply impressed with their importance and peculiar advantages. And why may not religion be among the blessings which they enjoy? When men for worldly interest flock together, as they do in these places, should not true Christians go with them to promote their eternal welfare?

"Let pass a few years and all the busy, bustling first settlers of these beautiful places will be in their graves. And what will be the character and destiny of those who occupy their places if nothing more be done than now appears to form their manners and their hearts anew?" Had the bishop been able to return not too many years later he would have found the little village bristling with churches of many denominations.

Four years after the bishop's visit, another unusual personage visited the village of Davenport. This time it was Prince DeJoinville of France, who occupied a suite at the LeClaire House, the area's finest hotel. It had been built in 1839 by Antoine LeClaire, founder of the City of Davenport.

The prince wrote of his American travels when he returned to France. He didn't mention his sojourn in Davenport, but recounted with obvious disgust his experiences in a hotel upriver in Galena, Ill. The prince noted that the hotel keeper added so many extras on the bill that, except for the accommodations, he would have imagined himself in one of Europe's most posh hotels.

The prince was particularly annoyed that one item on his bill included three dollars for just one tune played for his benefit on a piano. With royal pique, he declared, "and the tune was played with indifferent success!" □

An Episcopal bishop coming to visit Davenport? People in the slightly populated village barely wrested from the wilderness were agog in 1837 when they heard the news that Bishop Joseph Chase was on his way. Any visitors were rare, but such a high official of the church was even more of a wonder.

The bishop left notes of his visit. In them he expressed hope for the community's spiritual growth. His journal records that on July 13, 1837, he "came to that most pleasantly situated and rising village,

'LAND GRABBERS KEEP OUT'

The men in the finely-tailored clothes, diamonds sparkling on their fingers, were as much out of place among the rough and tumble pioneers in the Iowa Territory back in 1838 as if they'd come from another planet. They knew, too, that the muttering, roughly-dressed men from the woods and log cabins despised them and their reason for being there.

They were mostly Easterners, men the pioneers contemptuously dubbed "land-grabbers," and they had infiltrated the sparsely-settled Iowa Territory for one purpose — to make a killing in land. The pioneers, many of them desperately poor, knew the well-dressed gentlemen had not been around when they and their fathers were fighting and dying to wrest the land from a hostile wilderness. But they were there now to share the spoils — pockets and valises overflowing with silver.

◀

Drawing by Henry Lewis, Burlington, Iowa.

The first government land sale ever to be held in Iowa was conducted in Burlington, on the Mississippi River, and drew a strange assortment of men — speculators, money-lenders, settlers, and squatters. Burlington was then the capital of the Iowa Territory.

Out of the woods and from the remote river regions where they lived virtually alone, came those who had been there first, who had cleared the virgin lands and built their homes there. They were determined they would not give up all they had won without a fight. Yet for many, their only title was their labor upon the land. On paper, they had nothing to establish a claim.

The plain fact was that, regardless of what they'd done to it, the land was not theirs.

It belonged to the federal government, by virtue of treaties and conquest, and this day would be sold to the highest bidders. The sweat and blood of squatters didn't count as payment. Title to the land on a deed was the only thing that mattered. The speculators had no pity for the settlers. They would gladly buy a man's home from under him, or loan him the money to pay for the land at a staggering interest rate of 50 percent.

Most settlers had a common bond of poverty, and there was virtually no ready cash among them. Their only recourse, it seemed, was to borrow money at a rate almost impossible to repay, or to move on. The speculators, or land grabbers, came well prepared. One boat, loaded with silver coins to the water's edge, dodged floating ice cakes as it crossed the river from the Illinois shore and tied up in Burlington, Iowa. Capitalists from New York, Illinois and Ohio on that day lent $100,000 to settlers at the 50 percent interest rate.

Though they often squabbled among themselves, the settlers banded together against the common danger present at the land sale. Saving the land for which they'd worked so long and hard was an absolute necessity. The speculators, used to more genteel methods of doing business, were hardly prepared for the attitude of the hard-bitten pioneers. Each township present appointed one pioneer bidder to represent it. It was soon apparent to most of the would-be land grabbers that it would be extremely foolhardy to bid against any of these strange-looking men who kept their guns ever at their sides.

One speculator didn't get the message, though. He stood up, and in imperious tones, overbid the township representative.

Before he knew what had happened, he was knocked to the ground, pummeled and kicked, and dragged away protesting loudly. Those conducting the sale conveniently didn't seem to notice. The man probably would have been killed on the spot if some of the older settlers hadn't intervened. The speculator quickly withdrew his bid, and the land was sold at the settlers' price.

This was enough for the other land-grabbers present. They found it far safer to loan money at the high rates and to reap their profits from a distance. Except for that one incident, the land sale proceeded with no more interruptions. ☐

WARS OF WILDCAT WILSON

The men who wrested lands and fortunes from the pioneer wilderness had to be rough and rugged and ready to fight to keep what they'd won, but perhaps the toughest of all was a grizzled old piece of whang leather known as "Wild Cat" Wilson.

Few remembered his Christian name was John because he'd lived up to his "Wild Cat" reputation ever since he'd arrived in the new territory. It was said he could out-fight and out-drink any three men, and had never been known to back down from anyone or anything.

He and his sons made a living as claim-makers, staking out tracts of the virgin land and later selling them. They had established the claim that later became Rockingham, in what is now west Davenport. In the spring of 1836, they were making a claim on the edge of the prairie, along the old Blue Grass road from Davenport.

"Wild Cat" didn't know, and wouldn't have cared, that he was staking his claim across the trail the Indians used on their journeys to Col. George Davenport's trading post at Fort Armstrong. But one day as he was cutting trees for logs and hauling them with several oxen, some of Chief Black Hawk's braves came along on their way to the trading post.

The Indians hated all interlopers and stopped to warn "Wild Cat" Wilson he was trespassing on their land and interfering with their trail. They ordered him to leave the area immediately. "Wild Cat" always balked when anyone attempted to make him do anything. He was used to dealing with the Indians and was not afraid of them. He went right on with his work, surmising that after a certain amount of grumbling the Indians would move on, which they did.

But the braves returned after a few days in Davenport, and this time they were fortified with firewater from the trading post. When they arrived at the Wilson claim, they rode up the creek, turned their ponies loose, dropped their blankets from their shoulders, and prepared to enforce their demands for his departure.

The area was deserted except for "Wild Cat" and his two sons. As the Indians advanced, "Wild Cat" was some distance away chopping trees, but he came running when he heard his son, James, who had been driving the team, scream that the Indians were going to attack.

James jumped down from the wagon just as the second son, Samuel, arrived to help his father. "Wild Cat" didn't hesitate, but rolled up his sleeves,

Davenport 1854—From Rock Island Shore.

and with a spine-tingling "wild cat" yell, waded into the braves, striking those nearest him with his fists. The fact his family was outnumbered 14 to 3 apparently didn't bother him at all.

The Indians were surprised at the attack and fell back, but soon regrouped, and swarming over "Wild Cat" forced him to the ground. His sons, who had inherited their father's toughness, had no weapons, but quickly unhitched an ox and swung the heavy ox bow in a wide arc, knocking three Indians off their feet.

"Wild Cat" was up immediately and picked up the axe he'd dropped when the Indians attacked. Lifting it high over his head, he swung it as hard as he could, catching one of his attackers in the back and splitting him open from neck to belt line.

This was too much for the Indians. They picked up their dead and wounded and fled, while "Wild Cat" grunted, wiped off his axe, and went back to work. But the claim makers hadn't seen the last of the Indians.

The following Sunday they were back in greater numbers. As "Wild Cat" holed up in a neighbor's cabin, the Indians surrounded it, screaming for his scalp. It seemed there would be no way for the old man to escape, but the Indians didn't know a runner had already been sent to notify Antoine LeClaire, founder of the City of Davenport, and also Col. Davenport, of the Indians' actions.

These two men were highly respected by the Indians who considered their words to be law. When LeClaire said that they were to disperse and not bother "Wild Cat" again, or to cross his claim, they complied. Later they made a new trail from Davenport, running north through Little's Grove.

Never again did the Indians come near "Wild Cat's" claim, apparently believing what he had told Antoine LeClaire, "I'll scalp the first redskin who does!" □

A PIONEER CHRISTMAS

The winters were harsh and cruel and the land often hostile, but there was a warm, simple beauty in the Christmas observances of the Midwest pioneer settlers.

True, their lonely little cabins were often surrounded and isolated by deep snow, while wolves howled a mournful chorus in the woods, but inside a giant log would be glowing cherry-red in the fireplace, where the stockings hung nearby awaiting a visit from St. Nick.

Drawing by Henry Lewis. ▲

Mrs. Mary Miller, born in Clinton County, Iowa, in 1837, only nine years after the first white settlers entered the Black Hawk Purchase, once recounted the first Christmas she could remember in a little log cabin:

"In the morning we were gleeful at finding in each stocking a nice fat brown doughnut and some pieces of gaily-colored calico. I was very happy because I knew my elder sister would make and dress a rag doll for me, just like the one with which she played."

Game was plentiful and it was no great task to shoot a wild turkey for the Yule dinner. Maple sap had been gathered from an island in the Mississippi River, and mouth-watering mince pies simmered in the big Dutch oven. Berries had been gathered in the summer and dried. Home-rendered lard made the flaky pie crust even more tasty.

The pioneers, bound by their common lot, were usually quite friendly with one another. One practice on Christmas Eve was for a group of men to get together, elect one their "captain," and then tramp out to visit other neighborhood homes. When they arrived at a particular dwelling, the captain would loudly call out the man's name. The celebrants would then raise their muskets and fire a volley that echoed over the countryside.

With much merriment and back-slapping, the man of the house would invite his neighbors in, and his wife would set out pie and coffee for them. The men would reload their guns and set out for the next house. Often, all might join in a familiar hymn, and in some homes they'd gather for a devotional service. The visits would continue until midnight when Christmas was officially ushered in and the men would return to their homes and families.

Once the traditional Christmas feast was over, the youngsters, often accompanied by their parents, would put on their warmest clothing for a day of skating, coasting or sleighing. For many, Christmas Day was the traditional time for a well-organized hunting expedition. Balls and dances were often held on Christmas night.

More than 100 prairie wolves once set upon one Iowa group en route to a Christmas party, but the pioneers managed to outdistance them and soon forgot their fright as they sat down to a midnight supper of deer, elk, buffalo, cornbread, fried cakes and pumpkin pie.

In larger towns, such as Davenport, settlers often went to the local opera house or theater on Christmas Day. As communities grew and church congregations got larger, Christmas services featured Sunday school programs with children singing Christmas songs, giving recitations, and portraying the story of the Nativity.

The German settlers brought the concept of St. Nicholas to the Davenport area, as well as the Christmas tree with its toys, trinkets, figures of angels and lighted tapers.

One pioneer Iowa town reacted with wrath to a proposal to change Santa's traditional appearance. One citizen declared St. Nick should not appear as an "aristocratic gentleman of red-tape proclivities who with white kids and immaculate shirt bosom

A typical kitchen in a 19th century home.

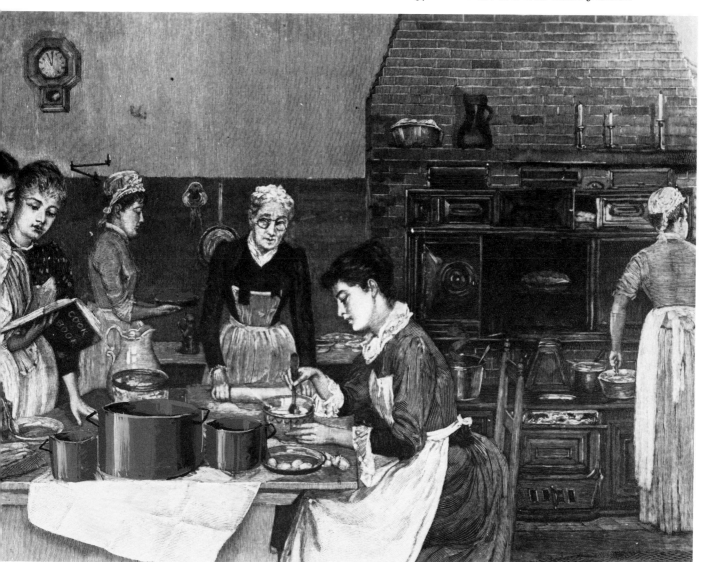

smiles benignly on the ladies, and daintly passes the presents from the tree to the eager expectants."

He added, "No, this modern Santa is not ours; ours is fat and merry and sooty. His shirt bosom won't bear inspection, neither are his pants a la mode. His medium circumference directly after dinner exceeds his altitude at noonday." □

FIRST DUEL IN IOWA

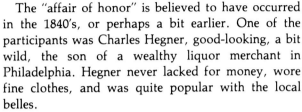

Hollywood couldn't have provided a better cast of characters for the first, and perhaps only, duel ever fought in Iowa. It was done with all the dash and verve two hot-blooded young men could supply, and though no one was killed, honor was considered satisfied.

The "affair of honor" is believed to have occurred in the 1840's, or perhaps a bit earlier. One of the participants was Charles Hegner, good-looking, a bit wild, the son of a wealthy liquor merchant in Philadelphia. Hegner never lacked for money, wore fine clothes, and was quite popular with the local belles.

His opponent was George Ralston, a well-to-do young gentleman of leisure, considered a bit foppish, but still sought after in social circles.

The two came together during a party at the old Rock Island House, a popular gathering place. As the young blades made frequent trips to the punch bowl, the talk got louder and the dancing faster. Suddenly angry voices arose above the din, and the dancers stood still. Both Hegner and Ralston had discovered that one of the young ladies, Miss Sophia Fisher, had promised to dance the same set with each of them.

Neither of the proud young men would relinquish what he considered to be his rights. Ralston declared coldly that he was going to have the dance and that Hegner could go to the devil!

"In that case, sir, I challenge you to a duel!" Hegner shouted, while a shocked murmur ran through the dancers.

"Your challenge is accepted, sir," Ralston replied as he whirled away with Miss Fisher. Given a choice of weapons, Ralston selected pistols at 20 paces. Ralston chose as his second, John Finch, a young writing school instructor, while Hegner secured the services of John Sperry, a dashing West Pointer, who assiduously avoided soldiering for pursuits closer to Hegner's. The duel was to take place on the banks of the Mississippi, a mile below Davenport. Dr. Craig of Rock Island agreed to be on hand as surgeon.

"The drinks are on me at the LeClaire House," Ralston declared.

"I'm at your service, sir," Hegner laughed, the matter of honor fully resolved. Dueling, however, was against the law and police took a dim view of the proceedings. When the duelists learned police were on their way to arrest them, they hurriedly downed their drinks and fled to Rock Island.

There they were met by Rock Island police who charged them with issuing a challenge on Illinois soil. Both were ordered to leave the county immediately or face arrest.

"I'm for a more civilized country where a man's honor is considered something of value," Ralston was heard to declare as the two left, arm in arm. □

The sun was just rising over the river as the duelists and their seconds arrived. A few townspeople were also present for the unusual event. One of the seconds then announced, "You will each walk 20 paces, turn and fire," and he began counting slowly as the men strode away from one another, cocked pistols at the ready.

"...Four, five, six," the voice intoned as Ralston suddenly turned around and asked, "Look, couldn't we settle this some other way? After all, it was only a dance."

But his opponent snarled, "Get on with it, I'll have nothing but your blood!"

"Then I won't kill you, but I'll wing you," Ralston threatened as he turned and walked on and the counting continued, until finally the voice ordered, "Fire!"

The two pistols boomed simultaneously. Hegner dropped his pistol and fell to the ground, shot in the right shoulder. Ralston, untouched, stood holding his smoking weapon, an anxious look on his face. Hegner was only slightly wounded and after Dr. Craig had dressed the arm, the two duelists shook hands.

GET OFF MY ROOF!

No one ever knew the real story of Capt. James R. Stubbs of Davenport, and a strange, improbable tale it was, too. The once brilliant Army officer and teacher became a recluse who lived in a riverbank cave with a weird assortment of domestic animals as his only companions.

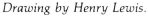

Drawing by Henry Lewis.

His intelligence was a certainty. Capt. Stubbs had graduated from West Point with high honors, and in 1822 was stationed at Fort Armstrong, later the site of the Rock Island Arsenal. The captain spent four years there, and his companions noted his fondness for the wild, untouched areas around the fort. Much of his off-duty time was spent in the woods and along the river.

Capt. Stubbs was transferred to the East in 1826, and later served for several years in the Post Office department. He also was much sought after as a private tutor. But something called him back to the untamed frontier country, and in 1833, he returned to the Davenport area.

Old friends were astonished at the change in Capt. Stubbs. He seemed to have lost all his spirit and was literally engulfed in melancholy. He seemed out of touch with reality and rarely spoke, even when spoken to. Some surmised he had had an unhappy love affair and had come back in the wilderness to brood about it. Others thought him insane.

Capt. Stubbs confided in no one, but began to drink heavily and to avoid all contact with others. Eventually he all but retired from the world, digging himself a cave in a secluded spot along the river in East Davenport, believed to be near the present site of Lindsay Park.

At first the townspeople buzzed about his strange behavior, but eventually they came to accept it and all but forgot him. Rivermen called the area in which the cave was located "Stubbs' Mound," and the general location, on a bend of the Mississippi River just below the chain of rocks at the foot of the Rock Island Rapids, was known as "Stubbs' Eddy."

For eight years, Capt. Stubbs inhabited the lonely cave, with no companions other than a pet pig, a cat and an occasional dog. These he treated as his "family," giving them stern lectures when they misbehaved. He would also hold "court" to mete out punishment to the guilty among them.

Residents would see him at morning, and again at night, as he marched along the river bank with his "family" following in military order. On his infrequent trips to town for supplies, Capt. Stubbs would often be accompanied by his pig and cat.

Once, in 1842, a newcomer to the area, A.C. Fulton, was walking along the river bank in East Davenport when he heard what seemed to be human speech coming from the ground. Astonished, Fulton stood and listened as a harsh voice delivered some sort of lecture.

When Fulton saw smoke issuing from what was Capt. Stubb's chimney, he called, "Hallo, what are you doing down there?"

There was an immediate reply, "What are you doing up there? Get off my house, sir." Fulton scrambled down and could hardly believe what he saw. There was a strange hermit surrounded by a troop of animals.

Fulton, who later became one of the recluse's few friends, learned he had stepped on the roof of the cave at the exact moment Capt. Stubbs was dressing down the pig for forgetting its manners and gulping a piece of cornpone its master had been saving for breakfast.

It seemed likely that Capt. Stubbs would live out his days in the cave, but, unexpectedly, after eight years he gave it up and moved back into a house. People surmised that the years of loneliness had deadened the hurt that made him become a hermit.

In time he ran for the office of justice of the peace and was elected, holding the post until his death in May, 1848. Nothing remains of Stubbs' cave today, just as nothing will ever be known of his reasons for inhabiting it. □

THREE KILLERS DIE

Bands played, children scampered excitedly about, and practically all of Rock Island trooped to an area a half block south of the county courthouse on that crisp fall day, Oct. 29, 1845. The event they had come to witness wasn't a parade or a political rally or a theatrical production, but the hanging of three of the men who had murdered Col. George Davenport in his home in Rock Island Arsenal. Everyone remembered the details of the slaying.

The rest of the old colonel's family had been in Davenport on July 4, 1845, attending an Independence Day celebration, but the master of the big home on the Arsenal had stayed home alone. Col. Davenport, for whom the city of Davenport was named, was thought by all to be very wealthy.

A group of cutthroats, believed to have had their headquarters in Nauvoo, Ill., downriver from Davenport, were known as the "banditti of the prairie," and they, too, had heard tales of the colonel's great wealth. Breaking into his home on that July 4th, they tortured him in an attempt to make him disclose where his money was hidden, though he insisted he had only a small amount in the house. The four men had hoped to escape with $100,000, but got only $400 or $500 and the colonel's watch and chain. Infuriated, they shot and mortally wounded the pioneer settler.

The gang was tracked down through some very clever detective work, and was discovered to have also terrorized settlers in six midwestern states. Col. Davenport was a very prominent man and the whole nation waited for word that the death sentence had been carried out against his murderers.

The area where the gallows was erected was in a natural bowl or amphitheater, selected because it would accommodate a large number of people. And the crowd gathered to watch the execution was estimated at 5,000, though the normal population of Rock Island was then only 1,660. Everyone who lived within riding or walking distance was there. Many were afraid to stay home alone because it was rumored the bandit gang would ride up to rescue their leader.

Colonel George Davenport, who lent his name to one of Iowa's great river cities, died at the hands of robbers.

But no help came as the sheriff arrived at 10 a.m., parading through the streets with his prisoners, accompanied by guards and music. A hollow square was formed around the prisoners at 12:30 p.m. by a guard of 130 men. The Green Mountain Boys, Rock Island's band, struck up a special dirge composed by George P. Abell, their director. It was intended, it was said, to "convey gloom, grief, distress, pain and the grave." The men to be hanged included John Long, his brother, Aaron, and Granville Young.

As the men stood on the platform looking out over the curious faces, Aaron Long and Granville Young asked, and received, permission to speak. Young appealed passionately to the crowd to come forward and rescue them, and many people in the crowd wept. Then the band played a hymn, and prayers were offered by the clergy. At 3:30 p.m., the noose was slipped over the head of one after the other, and each time the trap was sprung. When it was Aaron Long's turn the rope broke, and he had to be hanged again, but not before he had blurted out a confession to the murder.

His first words reportedly were "Don't choke a man and then hang him." They gave him a drink before they dropped him through the trap for the second and last time.

For many years, the skeleton of John Young hung in a glass case in the Rock Island County Courthouse, a grisly reminder of a dark day in Quad-City area history. Later, it was transferred to the John Hauberg Museum in Black Hawk State Park. It is still there today. ☐

REV. HUMMER'S BELL

The big old bell might have remained forever in the mud of the Iowa River at Iowa City if Brigham Young and his Mormons, making their long trek westward, hadn't found it and taken it with them.

This was just another twist in the strange story of the Rev. Michael Hummer, his church, and his remarkable bell that eventually spanned a continent.

As Iowa Citians strolled to church on Easter Sunday in 1842, they could smile contentedly as the rich tones of the big bell in the Old School Presbyterian Church called them to worship. If the congregation was fortunate to have such a fine bell, it was even luckier to have a devoted and industrious pastor like Rev. Hummer.

Rev. Hummer's life seemed to be a series of sudden stops and sharp turns. He was born in Kentucky in 1800, and at the age of 20 declared himself an atheist who would spurn spiritual rewards for the earthly pleasure of making money. Then abruptly, Rev. Hummer did an about-face, was converted, and eventually graduated from Princeton Theological Seminary.

In 1840, Rev. Hummer arrived in Iowa City and helped Launcelot Graham Bell, one of Iowa's pioneer Presbyterian preachers, organize the church there. The next year Rev. Hummer became the church's pastor, a post he filled with zeal and endless enthusiasm. When the congregation voted to build a church costing $5,500, Rev. Hummer was overjoyed.

He made three different trips to the East to collect money to help build the church. The amount he eventually raised isn't recorded, but he reportedly was to receive 10 percent of all he raised.

He returned singing from one trip, for in the back of his wagon was a real prize — a fine, big bell, which was eventually installed in the belfry of the new church.

From the start, the church seemed plagued with financial troubles and eventually this caused dissension between Rev. Hummer and his flock. Certain members of the congregation began to whisper that their pastor had become interested in Swedenborgianism, which they charged, involved some aspects of spiritualism. Ill-feeling reached such a point that Rev. Hummer left Iowa City and went to Keokuk, where he became actively associated with some Spiritualists. He still contended, though, that the Iowa City congregation owed him $600, which they were either unable or unwilling to pay. He demanded payment several times, but his pleas were not answered.

Hummer brooded about this and decided there was one thing that was still his — the bell. He vowed he'd reclaim it as partial payment of the debt. Accompanied by a friend, Rev. Hummer drove into Iowa City on a day late in 1848 and went directly to the church.

"Let them get their own bell," he told his friend, "This one is mine and I mean to take it back." The pastor clambered up a ladder, loosened the heavy bell, and began lowering it on a rope to the wagon below. But when he looked for his friend, he discovered the man, hearing that members of the congregation were approaching the church, had fled.

Members of the church quickly removed the ladder, leaving Rev. Hummer stranded high in the belfry. They loaded the bell on the wagon, whipped up the team, and drove off, while the pastor shouted useless threats.

Vowing to put the bell where the minister would never find it, members of the congregation drove directly to the Iowa River and sank the bell under several feet of water, after securing it with a rope to a nearby tree. The red-faced and very angry Rev. Hummer finally got down from the belfry, but search as he might, he never did locate the bell's watery hiding place.

Some time passed and a lot of people forgot about the bell. Then the long lines of Mormons, fleeing religious persecution in Nauvoo, Ill., passed through Iowa City on the way to their "Promised Land" in Salt Lake City. Some of the Mormons discovered the bell as they were sloshing across the river, and loaded it aboard one of their wagons. Eventually Rev. Hummer's bell went all the way to Salt Lake City.

Some time later, when Mormon leader Brigham Young learned that the bell was actually owned by the Iowa City church, he offered to return it, providing members would pay for its transportation.

But the offer was never accepted, and the bell was never returned. No one really knows for sure what ever did happen to it. □

A FOUR-MILE PAINTING

It's not unusual for an artist to spend weeks, months — even years — on a painting that will cover a small spot on a wall. Consider then, what a tremendous undertaking it would be to complete a painting four miles long!

Such a painting of the Mississippi River and the areas around it was finished, though, and, incredibly, it dwarfed a similar painting a mere three miles long. Easily the largest paintings in all history, both contained countless views of the Mississippi. And if they weren't the best works done on the subject, no one could dispute they were the longest.

The rest of the world knew little of the Mississippi in 1840, and five panoramists were drawn to the wild, untamed area. When 16-year-old John Banvard left New York, he had no resources and sparse training, but he burned with the ambition to complete the largest canvas. He took the first step toward fulfillment of the dream when he drifted down the Mississippi in a flatboat in the summer of 1836, awed at the ever-unfolding new scenic vistas. The youth spent five happy and creative years traveling up and down the river as a roving artist and peddler. His

Drawing by Henry Lewis. Fort Madison, Iowa.

notebook fattened with sketches of cities, forts, camps, landings, plantations, cliffs, points, bluffs and islands. When he felt he had enough, Banvard disappeared into a waterfront loft in Louisville, Ky., and was seldom seen thereafter. But in 1842, he announced that he had completed work on "Banvard's Panorama of the Mississippi." He proclaimed it on advertising posters to be "Painted on Three Miles of Canvas, exhibiting a View of Country 1,200 miles in Length, extending from the Mouth of the Missouri River to the City of New Orleans, being by far the Largest Picture ever executed by Man."

If it lacked anything in artistic skill, Banvard's painting was, nonetheless, something of a marvel. He rigged his canvas in such a way that he could unroll it before his audiences. When he showed it in river cities, audiences cheered as they spotted familiar landmarks. Banvard went east with his canvas, and arrived in time to help the poet Longfellow with his western scenes in "Evangeline."

The poet was grateful for the assistance, remarking, "The river came to me, instead of my going to the river." Banvard was triumphantly received in Boston, New York and Washington, D.C. where Congress passed a resolution praising his "wonderful and magnificent production." Off to Europe went Banvard, the three-mile canvas carefully stowed aboard ship. During the Christmas season in 1848, he displayed his painting in Egyptian Hall in Piccadilly. Among the crowds who flocked to see the work was author Charles Dickens, who praised its quality. Banvard reached the apex of his career when he gave a command performance for the Queen of England in Windsor Palace. He next began a tour of the Continent.

Unknown to Banvard, he had a rival, a young sign painter and carpenter named Henry Lewis, who had also been quite busy sketching the Mississippi. Traveling on the steamer Senator to St. Paul, Lewis recorded an area Banvard had missed, the Upper Mississippi.

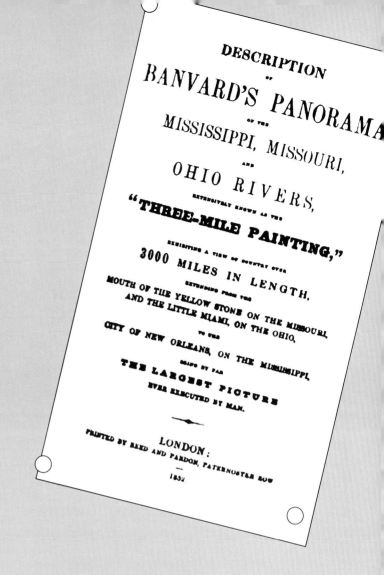

Lewis was even more ambitious. He envisioned a work that would be "a gigantic and continuous painting of the Mississippi River from the Falls of St. Anthony to where it empties into the Gulf of Mexico." To accomplish this gargantuan task, Lewis built a houseboat studio on a double keel provided by two strong canoes.

Lewis called his craft "Minnehaha" and equipped it with two small sails and a pair of heavy oars. When the weather was good, he could sit on his cabin roof and sketch. Moving leisurely, the young man battled mosquitoes, visited Indian camps and white settlements, studied islands, bluffs and headlands, and made hundreds of sketches.

What did they include? Such things as the broad waters of Lake Pepin, the lift of Maiden Rock and Trempealeau Mountain, the endlessly stretching Wabasha Prairie, the frescoed Piasan Rock, the Mormon tabernacle on the hill above Nauvoo, Ill., and the churches of Alton, under the wooded bluff.

Henry Lewis' sketch of his own activities and campsite along the Mississippi River.

Drawing by Henry Lewis.

Not content with mere scenery, Lewis usually included rivercraft in his drawings, and always named them, too. In the fall of 1848, he docked his boat and began his painting, which he would call the "Great National Work." The unveiling immediately knocked Banvard out of contention for having the world's longest painting. Lewis' was four miles long, a full mile longer than his rival's!

Lewis, like Banvard, showed his painting in various parts of the United States, and eventually toured Europe with it. He finally sold it to a Dutch planter who took it to Calcutta and later to Java. What happened to Lewis' painting after that isn't known, but Banvard's wound up eventually in Watertown, S.D., where he retired in the 1880's. Lashed up like a ship's canvas, it went into the cellar. A few years later, some portions of the canvas were used on the wall of a local building, finally disappearing forever under coats of varnish and wallpaper.

The works of Banvard and Lewis, though grandiose, were possibly not important, but they did serve to make the mighty Mississippi better known throughout the whole world. □

THE GREY EAGLE'S GREAT RACE FOR GLORY

Many are the legendary feats of the brash, courageous men who spent their lives on the mighty Mississippi River. King of the river in the early days was the steamboat, and colorful and determined were the crews who manned them.

Some of the deeds of these intrepid rivermen have become part of our song and folklore. For instance, everyone has heard of the famous race of the Natchez and the Robert E. Lee, and of the determination of "Steamboat Bill."

The Grey Eagle and two other ships at the boat mooring in St. Paul in 1859. (Buffalo Bill Museum Collection.)

An equally exciting race between two river behemoths has passed almost unheralded, the hell-bent scramble for glory between the swift Grey Eagle of Capt. Daniel Smith Harris, and the speedy packet Itasca, captained by David Whitten.

The Itasca, the ship that raced the Grey Eagle. (Buffalo Bill Museum Collection.)

On Aug. 6, 1858, the final splicing of the Atlantic Cable was completed in mid-ocean and the first message was flashed clear across the broad ocean. It was a triumphal achievement and there was much celebrating in the United States. Newspapers across the country vied with one another for "scoops" on the historic linkup. At this time, though, there was still one area of the country that was unlinked to the Atlantic Seaboard by telegraph, and still had to rely on the arrival of the steamboats for its news. That isolated area included St. Paul and river towns in Minnesota.

It was assumed that the packet boat, Itasca, then at Prairie du Chien, Wis., would be first to arrive in St. Paul with the momentous news. But when he heard the news at Dubuque, 65 miles downriver from the Itasca, Capt. Harris of the Grey Eagle decided he would be first, regardless of the odds.

Harris' ship and the Itasca were scheduled to leave their respective river ports at the same hour, 9 a.m., but the Grey Eagle would have to travel 265 miles and the Itasca only 200. Too, the Itasca had been setting new records for fast time. Carrying extra copies of the newspapers telling of the cable crossing and piling aboard every bit of combustible material — grease, butter and pitch—Capt. Harris set out from Dubuque to beat the Itasca.

By 9:30 p.m. he had reached Winona, Minn., which the Itasca had just left three-and-a-half hours before. Her nine hour lead had now been cut by two-thirds. This was despite the fact the Grey Eagle had also towed a wood flat for 20 miles before stopping to deliver it.

Capt. Harris detailed a deck hand to stand on the stage and heave the mail onto the bank at each landing as the boat chugged by at half speed. Freight was put off only where necessary and many passengers were induced to stay aboard until the race was over. Fire was shooting from the Grey Eagle's funnels at 4 a.m. the next day as she came rumbling up to the Red Wing levee, only 50 miles from St. Paul. However, the Itasca hadn't stopped at Red Wing, thereby gaining precious minutes. On and on, faster and faster, went the Grey Eagle, her big boilers straining.

At the Prescott levee, mail and freight were dumped out hastily. As the Grey Eagle roared past Point Douglas and over to Hastings, Capt. Harris could see the smoke of a boat rounding a bend two miles upriver. Through his glass he could see it was the Itasca!

Capt. Whitten of the Itasca up to that time had been unaware of Harris' intentions, but he quickly discerned them and ordered his engineer to pour on the fuel. Then the race was on in earnest!

Below Pine Bend, the Grey Eagle closed the gap to about a mile. By this time she was an amazing ten hours ahead of schedule. At Merrimac Island, the Grey Eagle, running like a race horse, was only three-quarters of a mile behind the Itasca, and at Newport only a half mile.

Now only a boat's length separated them as the boats shot through Kaposia, Pig's Eye, and Dayton Bluff. St. Paul was only one mile away. On the Grey Eagle's deck, the passengers cheered wildly. Slowly the bow of their boat drew abreast of the Itasca's stern. However, the Itasca had the inside track and it was soon clear Capt. Harris would be unable to reach the levee first.

Neck and neck the boats came into St. Paul, with whistles blowing and cannon booming. The Itasca nudged up to the dock first, but while her crew was putting out the stage, the Grey Eagle slid alongside.

Perched on a swinging stage, with a number of newspapers fastened into the notch of a large arrow of wood, was a deckhand. In a minute, Harris' agent on the dock caught them. Capt. Harris had managed to get the momentous news to St. Paul first! He had done something else, too.

He had made the run from Dubuque to St. Paul in 24 hours and 40 minutes, making 23 landings and taking on 35 cords of wood en route. His average speed, counting all stops, was a fraction over 11 miles an hour, but it is estimated the Grey Eagle made 13 miles an hour while underway. It was the fastest time ever made by a steamboat, beating the previous record by more than three hours.

Capt. Harris was accorded a hero's welcome in St. Paul and the fame of the Grey Eagle was known the length and breadth of the "Father of Waters." □

THE PROPHET'S DOWNFALL

The fanaticism of the man almost defied belief, yet there were those in the little Bishop Hill colony near Galva, Ill., who were willing to follow him and entrust him with their lives.

Who was this man who at one time, irked with God, threatened to depose Him from heaven "for you cannot reign without me?" His name was Eric Janson, a man who called himself "Prophet" and the "vicar of Christ on earth."

He was a poor boy, born in Sweden, and eventually he became the spiritual leader of a little religious colony in the New World, a self-professed omnipotent leader whose word was absolute law for his followers. He once told his people, "All authority has been granted unto me in heaven and on earth. If I so willed, you would at once fall dead at my feet and go to hell!"

Today, Bishop Hill is a prosperous farming community. It was founded in 1846, and in the four years that he led and commanded it, the Prophet Janson stamped every facet of its life with his overpowering personality. Janson visualized a virtual Garden of Eden for his people, but their life was incredibly hard. He had no idea that the vision was already doomed the day a young soldier of fortune named John Root rode into the colony. A member of a wealthy Stockholm family, Root had been serving with the U.S. Army in Mexico.

Janson at first welcomed the newcomer, but took an intense dislike to him when he began to court the Prophet's cousin, Charlotte Louise. Eventually he agreed to their marriage, but only on condition the girl would remain in the colony if Root ever decided to leave.

An epidemic of cholera swept the little colony in 1849. Charlotte Louise was expecting a child, and her husband insisted she leave with him. When she refused, in accord with Janson's wishes, Root left alone. Their son was born on Oct. 25 and was named John, after his father. Months later, when Root learned of his son's birth, he returned to Bishop Hill and attempted to take his wife and child away with him. They were intercepted by colonists a short distance from the settlement and forced to return.

Terribly angry, Root obtained a court order charging Janson and other colonists with "riot."

While his wife was in Cambridge, Ill., for the hearing, Root abducted her and took her to Chicago, but the colonists found her there and took her back to Bishop Hill.

The situation became more tense on March 25, 1850, when 70 men led by Root rode into the colony, intending to take Mrs. Root away by force. However, she had already left for a place of safety, after filing an affidavit in which she stated she feared her husband would kill her. The armed mob roamed through the streets of the colony, threatening to burn the homes and kill the inhabitants, according to one account.

During the night they entered every house, searching vainly for Mrs. Root. The following day they returned, ripped boards off the church and some of the homes, fired their guns, and ordered colonists to leave their homes so they could burn them. Men of the colony were ordered into the church basement, while the women and children were held captive in the hospital.

Not knowing whether they would be killed or their homes destroyed, the residents of Bishop Hill spent long agonizing hours in suspense before they were finally released. The next day the mob rode back into the settlement to burn haystacks. They also, unaccountably, set fire to buildings at Little Hill near Cambridge.

Janson had been absent during this time, but returned from St. Louis on May 11, 1850. He immediately mounted the pulpit and delivered a sermon fraught with foreboding and a presentiment of death.

Standing before his followers, the Prophet quoted this passage: "I am already being offered and the time of my departure is come. I have fought the good fight, I have finished my course, I have kept the faith." Many of his followers wept and prayed for their leader.

The next day Janson left for the courthouse in Cambridge where he was the defendant in ten cases involving colony financial dealings. Many wondered at his final words, spoken almost in jest as he rode away, "Will you stop a bullet for me today?"

The May term of court was in session and the courthouse was packed. Also there was John Root, determined to force a showdown on the fate of his wife and child. He stomped up to Janson and demanded that his wife be returned.

The Prophet's imperious reply infuriated Root, who drew a pistol and fired, the bullet striking Janson just above the heart. The Prophet slumped to the floor and was dead within five minutes. Root was immediately arrested and charged with murder by a grand jury that convened the same day. Back to Bishop Hill went a sad little entourage, bearing the body of the fallen leader.

Root claimed he had fired in self defense, a statement apparently at least partly believed, because he was charged with the lesser crime of manslaughter and was sentenced to just two years in prison. He served 18 months and died shortly after his release.

The shot fired by Root not only killed the self-styled Prophet of Bishop Hill, but marked the beginning of the end in an ill-fated experiment in communal living. ☐

Typical of the trains of the early period of railroading. (Putnam Museum Collection.)

A MAGNIFICENT EXCURSION UP THE MISSISSIPPI RIVER

There were railroad coaches and locomotives festooned with flowers, flags and streamers — notables from every walk of life, including a former president of the United States — a flotilla of steamboats maneuvering up the Mississippi River like an armed squadron.

Is it any wonder they called it "the most magnificent excursion, in every respect, which has ever taken place in America?"

From all over the United States came captains of industry, leading historians and educators, grand society dames, all to help celebrate a tremendous achievement — the completion of the first railroad to unite the Atlantic Ocean with the Mississippi.

The historic linkup occurred in Rock Island, Ill. on Feb. 22, 1854. Contractors for construction of the Chicago and Rock Island Railroad invited hundreds of people to take part in a joint railroad-steamboat excursion from Chicago to Rock Island, and thence to the Falls of St. Anthony as Minneapolis was then called.

Preparations for the mammoth excursion were so elaborate that an eastern newspaper said they "could not be rivaled by the mightiest among the potentates of Europe." The most distinguished traveler was former President Millard Fillmore, but the rest of the assemblage read like a "Who's Who in America."

The excursionists left the Rock Island station in Chicago on June 5 aboard two trains of nine coaches each all gaily decorated and drawn by powerful engines.

At every stop, the travelers were greeted with

Union Station and dock in St. Paul. Here America's two greatest means of early transportation were joined. (A & A Coins, Stamps, and Collectables.)

speeches, military parades and booming cannon salutes. On hand in Rock Island to greet the visitors and take them on the Mississippi River portion of their journey, were the steamboats "Golden Era," "Spar Hawk," "The Lady Franklin," "The Galena," and "War Eagle." However, there were so many unexpected or uninvited guests that two more craft, the "Jenny Lind," and the "Black Hawk" had to be chartered.

Even then, there wasn't enough room for everyone. Staterooms had been allotted in Chicago where the names had been registered, but many of the tickets had been lost, and some passengers had none

Typical steamboat of the period. (A & A Coins, Stamps, and Collectables.)

at all. Through errors, some husbands and wives were assigned to different boats. About a third of the excursionists gave up in disgust and returned to Chicago, but 1,200 jammed aboard the steamboat flotilla.

Prior to departure, the passengers were entertained with a brilliant fireworks display. Then with bells ringing and whistles sounding, the boats, decorated with prairie flowers and evergreens, puffed away upstream with bands blaring on their decks.

Shortly after midnight a violent storm broke upon the river. Nothing could be seen, but occasional flashes of lightning illuminated the seven bobbing steamboats, slowly feeling their way through the churning waters. The storm subsided within a few hours.

Many of the passengers, used to the finest accommodations, slept on mattresses on the decks. Nobody got much sleep, either, since the mattresses could not be put down until midnight, and had to be removed by 5 a.m. so breakfast could be served. Large throngs greeted the armada whenever it stopped to "wood up", or take on fuel. Many times the boats were lashed together and passengers crawled back and forth, visiting old friends and meeting new ones.

A newspaper account called the appearance of the fleet as it rounded the bend below St. Paul "grand beyond precedent." The steamboats approached with two full bands playing lively airs. The excursionists were hustled into every type of conveyance for the trip to the Falls of St. Anthony. After touring the area and feasting with the inhabitants, the excursionists returned to their boats for the downriver trip.

The meals served on board were fit for any gourmet, and included such things as speckled trout, oysters and lobsters in sealed cans, hens, turkeys and ducks. Two cows on the lower decks provided fresh milk each morning, and there was an infinite variety of desserts.

Like the other notables who made the journey, Fillmore was lavish in his praise of the Upper Mississippi steamboats. He declared the excursion was one for which "history has no parallel, and such as no prince could possibly undertake."

Historian George Bancroft later dwelt at length upon the fact that more than 1,000 people had easily and safely been transported a distance greater than from New York to Liverpool.

The New York Tribune seemed to sum up the feeling of most of the excursionists when it urged travelers to follow "in the wake of the just completed railroad excursion, ascend the Upper Mississippi, the grandest river of the world, flowing for a thousand miles between shores of incomparable beauty — the boundaries of states destined to wealth, population and power almost without rival in the Union." □

One of the earliest of the posters used to advertise the schedule. This one, from 1855, is carefully preserved under glass at the Putnam Museum in Davenport.

NIGHTMARE BROUGHT LOCOMOTIVE

Maybe it was something Charlie Slack ate before going to bed one night in 1854 that produced the nightmare responsible for bringing the first railroad locomotive to Iowa long before anyone thought it possible. How could a nightmare move a locomotive? It happened like this:

No bridges spanned the mighty Mississippi River in the mid-1800's. Trains could run as far as Rock Island, and there they stopped. What was obviously needed to open the whole west to rail traffic and settlement was a bridge across the wide, treacherous stream, but getting one built was a major problem.

Slack was chief engineer for the railroad that began to lay track in Iowa, from the river westwards, in 1853, anticipating the day the bridge would be completed. The railroad brought in 2,000 workers from the east, and they were making good

progress before the line ran out of money with the trackage still incomplete. There was no cash for the men, but they were given food and dry goods from the company stores. So many bolts of cloth were given in lieu of money that workers sarcastically referred to the line as the "Calico Road."

Even before the line from Davenport to Iowa City was completed, it was evident there would be one major flaw in its operation, even if all the tracks were laid. The railroad had no locomotive on the Iowa side — and how could it get one there without a bridge across the Mississippi?

Engineer Slack was one of the men most troubled by the problem. One night as he dropped into fitful slumber, he had a terrible nightmare.

Slack dreamed that a smoking, snorting locomotive was pursuing him across the Mississippi, intent upon devouring him. In his dream, Slack jumped desperately from one ice floe to another, with the demonic locomotive huffing right behind him. Slack woke up terrified and wild-eyed, but as he reviewed the dream in his mind, he shouted, "By golly, that's it!"

It was so simple he wondered that he hadn't thought of it before. The locomotive could slide across the ice from the Illinois to the Iowa shore. He could pick the coldest day when the ice would be very thick and perfectly safe. And that is just how the first locomotive arrived in Iowa.

◀

Portion of a stereoptican view of the first bridge across the Mississippi at Davenport. (Putnam Museum Collection.)

Eventually the railroad got enough money to complete the line to Iowa City, and it was a gala day when the first locomotive arrived there. Everyone turned out for the biggest celebration in the town's history. They watched and waited, and just at dusk, streaming black smoke and proudly tooting its whistle, the little locomotive chugged into view.

Every resident had placed a candle in a window to light up the streets. Bands played and people cheered. A huge-four-layer cake, baked in honor of the occasion, had demanded every fresh egg in the county. Iowans could now boast that they had 50 miles of completed railroad track in their state.

■

Reproduction from a John Deere calendar of the 1930's depicts the celebration opening the first railroad bridge across the Mississippi. (Iowa City Historical Society Collection.)

Meanwhile, work was progressing on the all-important link, the bridge over the Mississippi between Davenport and Rock Island. As it reached the stage of final completion, it was viewed by large crowds. A derrick swung out a crude, ironbound wooden girder which was lowered slowly and ponderously until at last, it touched both ends of the unfinished span.

It was a great moment in history and people on both sides of the river cheered themselves hoarse. For the first time, the "Father of Waters" had been bridged. By 1856, the last couplings were completed and a train proceeded carefully over the bridge and into Davenport.

It was a marvel of engineering for its day, stretching 1,580 feet. It had cost $400,000, small by today's costs, but an enormous sum for those times. To assure that larger boats could continue to navigate the Mississippi, the center span was designed to swing open. Soon, trains carrying thousands of eager immigrants started to arrive.

Iowans were justifiably proud, but downriver in St. Louis, Mo., the merchants were furious. They were certain they would now be by-passed by all of the rich trade between east and west. To combat this slight, they formed "Stop the Bridge" clubs. Even far-off New Orleans was concerned about the economic implications of the crossing, and called the bridge "the work of the Devil."

Citizens in the two southern cities even brought suit in federal court, seeking to halt use of the bridge. For months the case dragged on. The bridge had been in operation only a short time when the steamer Effie Afton crashed into the middle pier, sinking the boat and setting the western section of the span afire. Repairs were made to the bridge, but steamboat interests again took up the cry that the bridge was a menace to navigation and should be abolished.

In 1859, Abraham Lincoln, then a young lawyer, pleaded before the courts that erection of the bridge was entirely within the law. There was complicated legal wrangling that often seemed to be going against the span, but finally it won grudging acceptance and played a major role in the opening of the West. □

HE WOULDN'T STAY HANGED

Horses were so important to the early Scott County settlers that the ultimate penalty — death — was often decreed for anyone brash enough to steal one and careless enough to get caught.

And it was for both of those reasons, on a Fourth of July day in 1857 that a red-faced man named Orrie Teeples stood under a big oak tree in Davenport, on the verge of losing not only his independence, but his life. The impromptu "necktie party," without benefit of judge or jury, was being staged by an aroused group called the Vigilantes of Scott County.

It was pretty certain that Teeples' rough-shod feet had never walked over the floor of a church, but as he stood under the waiting branch of the oak, with a rope knotted behind his ear, he prayed in his own clumsy way, though it didn't seem possible anything could save him.

An outbreak of horse thievery had stirred farmers in the Hickory Grove Road area northwest of Davenport to form their own volunteer vigilante force. In times of emergency such groups acted much as volunteer fire departments do today. The pioneers feared the horse thief even more than the Indians, most of whom were relatively friendly by this time, because he took their only form of transportation. They felt horse thieves deserved the stiffest penalty they could hand out.

When the farmers caught Teeples sneaking out of the pasture with a horse on the end of a rope, his fate was already sealed as far as they were concerned. They held their own trial right there, and, as expected, the death penalty by hanging was decreed.

There was no appealing the verdict, either, as Teeples knew while he waited, alternately cursing and praying, for the vigilantes to carry out the sentence. Three men held his arms while the end of the rope was thrown over the branch above. Several vigilantes then tugged on the rope until they had lifted Teeples, kicking and squirming, several feet off the ground. There they left him to die — or so they thought.

Leaving the hanging scene, the vigilantes encountered some of Teeples' unsavory colleagues and told them of his predicament, hoping they would be impressed with the fate waiting all horse thieves in Scott County. They advised the men to cut Teeples' body down and bury it.

The friends hurried to the tree, and, sure enough, there was Teeples hanging by his burly neck. Only he wasn't dead, in fact, far from it. He was still kicking and squirming at the end of the rope. In their haste to hang Teeples, the vigilantes apparently had fashioned an ill-fitting noose. Teeples, who reportedly had a neck as broad and strong as a bull's, had merely feigned death. His neck was unbroken and his only injury was slight rope burns. But before he could enjoy the sensation of literally returning from the dead, the vigilantes returned, amazed to see their horse thief still alive.

It was not only disconcerting, but it presented a dilemma. A man who was hanged was expected to stay hanged, not to come back to life. Was it divine intervention, an answer to Teeples' hasty prayers? The vigilantes didn't concern themselves with that, but prepared to string Teeples up again.

This time Teeples begged for his life with the fervor of a man possessed, promising to disclose the names of all the horse thieves with whom he was associated, a promise that caused the very hasty departure of the friends who had cut him down. From Teeples' trembling lips tumbled the names of horse thieves, counterfeiters and other evil-doers. By this time some of the vigilantes had had time to think it over and to wonder if it were really playing the game to hang a man twice.

There was considerable argument from both sides, while Teeples stood, by, breathing heavily and rolling his eyes beseechingly. Finally the vigilantes marched him to the county line, shoved him across, and vowed if he ever showed his face again, they'd make certain next time the knot was tied properly. They say Orrie Teeples set some kind of record for getting out of sight.□

JOHN BROWN IN DAVENPORT

Nobody paid any attention to the big bearded stranger who strode purposefully down the street in Davenport on Independence Day in 1859 and turned into Teele and Dalzell's grocery store. Everyone was busy celebrating the holiday and most stores in town were closed.

Teele only nodded as the stranger looked about imperiously and inspected the goods. The grocer did notice that the stranger's long hair seemed to fly in every direction, that he had a very full beard, and wore clothing of an old-fashioned cut.

Teele rushed up as the customer cleared his throat.

"Yes sir," he asked, "is there something I can do for you?"

The stranger gave him a long, piercing look. "Yes, he finally replied, "has thee any sidemeat?"

"No," Teele admitted, "we are just out of sidemeat, but we do have some fine shoulders."

"I did not ask thee for shoulders," the stranger said gruffly. "I asked for sidemeat."

Not wanting to lose the sale, Teele suggested the stranger accompany him to Burr and Swift's store, which was also open, and where sidemeat might be available. An ample supply was on hand, and the stranger made a large purchase. Then he returned to Teele's store where he ordered more than $400 worth of provisions.

Teele was naturally delighted with making such a large sale, especially on a holiday, but there was something about the stranger that bothered him. Maybe it was the way in which he made everything he said sound like a command. Perhaps, thought Teele, he was a former army officer or wealthy businessman, though he certainly didn't look like the latter.

The grocer helped the stranger carry the provisions to a huge conestoga wagon whose high bed flared forward and backward like the ends of a scow. All the provisions were stored under the cover. When the loading was completed, the stranger flicked the reins and drove off without a word.

Piled atop the provisions were the wooden boxes containing the sidemeat. Each was stamped "Burr & Swift, Davenport, Iowa." The boxes, and the bearded stranger were to play a role in an incredible historic event.

They would next turn up at Harper's Ferry where the bearded man would be caught, tried and hung. His name was John Brown. Brown was a zealot who was certain he had been chosen by God to raid the arsenal at Harper's Ferry. He had many followers and hoped to spur an uprising among the slaves.

He took the provisions bought in Davenport to Springdale, a small settlement near Iowa City and Tipton. His men were there, training for the Harper's Ferry raid. Brown had chosen that quiet community because many of the Quakers there were sympathetic to his cause.

The Quakers felt that Brown embodied their own sentiments against slavery and allowed him to live there and drill his men for the coming raid. Brown insisted on a rugged training schedule.

■ ═══════════════════════════════

His men were up at five each morning, and immediately after breakfast they studied books on military tactics. After that came long periods of outside drill. The afternoon brought gymnastics and company maneuvers, including practice with wooden sabers. Twice weekly the men met in "mock legislative" sessions to discuss and vote upon topics of the day.

One of the weighty questions upon which they voted was the resolution that: "John Brown is more justly entitled to the sympathy and honor of this nation than George Washington."

A few months after his visit to Davenport, Brown and his men moved out to conduct the raid. The arsenal at Harper's Ferry was hit on Oct. 16, 1859. Brown was captured by the militia near the same wagon in which his provisions were stored.

Government investigators found the boxes bearing the name of the Davenport store, and sent agents to the city to see if they might round up some of Brown's collaborators. It was only then that Davenporters realized who their bearded visitor had been.

□

■

GHOSTS IN THE CLOCK TOWER?

If restless ghosts haunt the Clock Tower Building on Rock Island Arsenal, it would not be strange because the structure was completed in part with materials that once formed the island prison where 1,961 Confederate soldiers died of disease.

The bloody battles of the Civil War were still in progress when Major C.P. Kingsbury of the Army Ordnance Department arrived on Aug. 13, 1863, to take command of the new Rock Island Arsenal. Congress on July 11, 1862, had passed an act establishing national arsenals at Columbus, Ohio, Indianapolis, Ind., and at Rock Island. Major Kingsbury's instructions included detailed plans for construction of the storehouse which would later be known as the Clock Tower Building, long one of the Arsenal's most imposing landmarks.

The building had a troubled beginning. Major Kingsbury first found it difficult to obtain needed materials. Too, many private citizens claimed various rights and privileges to portions of the island on which the Arsenal was to be constructed. By Sept. 1, 1863, these difficulties had been ironed out and construction of the Clock Tower, first permanent building on the island, was begun. During the summer and fall of 1863, work was begun on another project—a prison designed to hold 13,000 Confederate prisoners of war. The Civil War delayed construction of the Main Building, as it was then called, and the "Clock Tower" wasn't completed until 1867.

Sandstone for the building came from a former quarry at LeClaire, Iowa. The massive stone blocks were transported down the Mississippi River to the west end of the island. The Clock Tower Building was originally designed as a storehouse for the Arsenal, with a headquarters building planned to occupy a site on higher ground to the south. Officially the Clock Tower was then referred to simply as "Storehouse A." The headquarters and other buildings planned for the west end of the island were never constructed there because the Arsenal was moved farther east, near the center of the island.

Into the Clock Tower went wood from the original Fort Armstrong, as well as material from the former Confederate prison camp, the latter being used mostly for window frames in the building's basement. The tower on the north side of the building is 25 feet square and 117 feet high. The six-foot hands on the clocks sweep across 12-foot dials facing in all four directions. The striking bell, which tolls each hour, weighs 3,500 pounds and can be heard all over the Arsenal. The Clock is wound once a week.

Major Kingsbury supervised excavation operations for the Clock Tower Building, as well as construction of the basement and part of the first floor. Then he left for another assignment and Bvt. Brig. Gen. Thomas J. Rodman assumed command of the Arsenal. Gen Rodman, who is buried on the Arsenal, is known as the "Father of the Arsenal." Under his command, the Clock Tower Building was completed, and other Arsenal buildings partially finished. One mystery is why the date of 1865 appears on the Clock Tower Building, since that is not the date it was completed, or when the cornerstone was laid.

Nor was the building constructed according to original plans. Greater thickness was added to the walls, the gable roofs were raised for additional storage space, and a face was added to the clock. The Clock Tower Building, contrary to some reports, never served as a headquarters for the Arsenal. It was used for receiving and issuing military equipment, from its completion in 1871 until 1930 when it became vacant. In 1932, the basement was used by the Army Engineers as a project office while the nearby Lock and Dam No. 15 was under construction. Finally renovated, the building became headquarters of the Rock Island District Corps of Engineers in 1934, when the district office was moved from the former Rock Island Post Office building. The Clock Tower still performs that function today.

At one time, the government ordered the building razed, and only strong protests from Quad-City residents caused the order to be rescinded. Sometime before 1932, lightning struck the building, setting a fire that caused considerable damage.

Most of the soil around the building was removed in 1869 to form the nearby Rock Island Railroad Lines embankment. Grading the soil away left the Clock Tower, which rests on a solid rock foundation, one to one-and-a-half feet higher than it had been originally. That the old building could actually "grow" seems consistent with its legend. □

ALL ABOARD THE STAGE!

One of the important men of his day, who somehow seems to have escaped the glamour with which America endowed most of its early folk heroes, was the intrepid stagecoach driver. Western movies rarely show him in anything but a rather menial role, and accounts of his heroism and rugged individuality are virtually non-existent.

But an important man he was, and early settlers accorded the driver of the stage the deference that was his due. He cut a dashing figure, too, as he sat, reins looped about his fingers, on the elevated driver's seat of the rumbling old Conestoga stage as it creaked into town after town behind four spirited horses.

The stagecoach driver was captain of his craft, just as the steamboat captain was master of his boat. The driver's word was law, and if a passenger was ordered to leave the stage, he did so immediately if he was wise. The driver was tremendously proud of his horses, and anyone who made derogatory remarks about them was inviting instant mayhem. Because the driver carried the U.S. mail, he demanded, and got, right-of-way over all other coaches and wagons.

Main stage routes in Iowa were from Dubuque to Cedar Falls, Dubuque to Iowa; Clinton to Cedar Rapids; Davenport to Council Bluffs by way of Des Moines; Davenport to Cedar Rapids; Burlington to Des Moines by way of Mount Pleasant, Fairfield, Ottumwa and Oskaloosa; Keokuk to Keosauqua, and Oskaloosa to Council Bluffs.

These main lines were connected by routes running north and south from Cedar Falls to Cedar Rapids, Iowa City to Keokuk, and from Dubuque to Keokuk by way of Davenport, Muscatine and Burlington. The Western Stage Co. was the state's largest operator, using more than 1,500 men, 3,000 horses and 600 coaches. Its capital investment was a million and a half dollars, a mighty sum in those early days.

Among the stagecoach companies competition was fierce, especially when they traveled the same routes. Not only did this result in frequent rate cuts in an attempt to woo passengers, but in races in which each driver sought to outdo the other. Sometimes rates plunged so low that passengers could travel long distances for almost nothing, with meals and lodging thrown in free.

Last word in luxury in its day was the Concord coach, oval in shape, but flattened on top to carry baggage. The oval body rocked on flexible braces. Of course, the passengers rocked, too, and were considerably shaken up at the end of a long journey.

Stagecoach drivers were great show-offs and it was customary for a coach to arrive and depart with a flourish involving great shouting and whip-snapping. The driver was a mighty, haughty man to whom it was deemed quite a privilege to speak. One driver, Ansel Briggs, operated a stagecoach in Iowa, settled in Andrew, and later became the state's first governor.

Old Clock Tower in the Rock Island Arsenal photographed about 1915. (Photo from the Public Information Office, Rock Island Arsenal.)

Iowa City Historical Society Collection.

On the road, the driver had to be many things — look-out, pilot, captain, conductor, engineer and mechanic. He had to know every hill, bump and rut and be able to make repairs in out-of-the-way places.

In addition, he had to contend occasionally with balky horses, bandits, and complaining passengers. A trip from Fort Madison to Keokuk was described by writer A. Cunynghame:

"...The road was dreadful; no one can imagine what a bad road is until he has traveled in the western states of America. The coaches are so constructed that they will ride easily over almost any obstacles, and from their immense strength they will resist any shock, however severe.

"...When quite full I cannot say that they are very agreeable, and when nearly empty the unfortunate inmate is thrown about like a parched pea on a drum. The body is hung on very substantial leather straps, and the baggage is stowed at the rear, in a sort of rack or cradle, which is wrapped over with leather covering to defend it from the weather."

It was the practice of some stage lines to charge more for overweight passengers, mainly on the theory they took up more space and their extra weight was harder to pull. The rate in Iowa generally varied from five to seven cents a mile. The stage

arrived and left when it got there. Roads were so bad and breakdowns so frequent that fixed schedules were almost impossible to maintain.

The country in those days hadn't been surveyed and early roads didn't follow section lines, but generally took the paths of easiest resistance or stuck to the high ground on ridges. When one track became impassable due to ruts, another was started.

One writer had this to say of stage travel: "When the roads are settled, this is a tolerable route (Iowa City to Council Bluffs). But in the spring, the roads are under the special direction of the devil, assisted by the Western Stage Co."

He commented further: "I must say the arrangements of this company are villainously poor. Crows look with secret satisfaction upon its horses. The coaches are poor; the drivers swear like the Devil; while the sleeping and eating along the route is neither more nor less than nasty.

"That these representations are true, I refer to the testimony of many thousands who have been hauled, mauled, squeezed, starved and humbugged (and we might add bedbugged) along this route."

Stagecoach travel wasn't all glumness and discomfort, though. There were some smooth roads, plenty of time to strike up conversations, huge meals at some stops, occasional nips from a bottle of good cheer, and many a tall tale spun.

The stage lines quite naturally prompted the growth of hotels and eating places along their routes. Muscatine had a number of these, among them Robert C. Kinney's "Iowa House," an estab-lishment that also served, improbably, as a place of worship, hospital and amusement hall.

Capt. James Palmer maintained a hostelry known far and wide as "Capt. Jim's." There one could get board and room for three dollars a week, or a big meal for just 25 cents. The stagecoach lines flourished until almost the end of the 1860's. By then the iron horse was snorting over its rails and the end was in sight. Stage schedules and terminals were shifted to make connections with the railroads.

The proud Western Stage Co. threw in the towel on July 1, 1870, junking its $1,000 Concord stages for as little as $10 apiece, and selling its horses. A colorful era of American history was over. □

DEATH ON THE ARSENAL

The hundreds of citizens huddled behind rope barricades in the 32-below zero temperature of Dec. 3, 1863, were waiting to see a rare sight—the arrival of thousands of Confederate soldiers captured by Gen. U.S. Grant's men in the recent battles of Lookout Mountain and Missionary Ridge.

The Rebels were being brought to occupy the new prison barracks on Rock Island Arsenal Island. The crowd watched in silence as the prisoners' train was switched off at a point on the Arsenal, and the 5,592 Confederate soldiers disembarked and slowly formed into uneven columns. They stood, forlorn and hopeless, shivering and nearly freezing in the bitter, unaccustomed cold.

Even as they were marched to their fence-enclosed compound, many of the Confederates were deathly ill with the dread disease, smallpox. In the coming month, that and other diseases would decimate their ranks even more than had the shot and shell of the battlefield.

Inspecting the Confederate prisoners at the Rock Island Arsenal during the Civil War. (Public Information Office, Rock Island Arsenal.)

Their barracks were surrounded by a rough board fence 12 feet high. Four feet from the top of the fence was a boardwalk for the guards. There was a sentry box every 100 feet. The stockade fence stretched for 1,300 feet to the east and west, and 900 feet north and south. Construction of the prison had begun in late August of 1863, and by Oct. 15 of that year it was ready to receive prisoners. But no sooner had the beaten Confederate soldiers arrived, than post surgeons found themselves faced by a terrible problem. There were 94 cases of smallpox in the first group, and all had been exposed to it. Lacking a hospital, surgeons took over certain barracks in the southwest portion of the stockade for that purpose. A "pest house" was erected on the island's south shore about a half mile from the prison proper. There was no effective medicine to combat smallpox, though, and by the end of December almost 100 Confederates had died and been buried about 400 feet directly south of the prison. The toll kept climbing grimly, 231 dead in January, 346 in February. Medical men began to wonder if perhaps the diseased dead had been buried too close to the prison, and after March 1 all who died were buried in the present location of the Confederate Cemetery on Arsenal Island. Those who had first died were later transferred to the cemetery.

Eventually Arsenal officers erected a hospital for non-contagious diseases on the site of the present Arsenal shops. Pest houses were built on the south shore and all soldiers or prisoners suffering from smallpox were removed from the prison enclosure. The prison camp was constructed in a low, swampy area, but a sewage system was built for better drainage and sanitation, and an adequate water supply was installed.

Government records show rations issued the prisoners were the same as those given Union troops, except that the Confederates received two ounces less per ration of meat and bread. Col. Johnson, whom one former prisoner later labeled "as inhuman a brute as ever disgraced the uniform of any country," explained the disparity in rations was due to the fact that the prisoners performed no labor, while his troops worked hard.

Col. Johnson gave some insight into his personal feelings, though, after the Rock Island Argus newspaper editorially accused him of mistreating and starving the prisoners. He replied in a letter to the editor:

"I have no objection to give you, in plain terms, what would be my action in regard to the treatment of prisoners in my charge if discretionary power rested with me: In the first place, instead of placing them in fine, comfortable barracks, with three large stoves in each and as much coal as they can burn, both day and night, I would place them in a pen with no shelter but the heavens, as our poor men were at Andersonville.

"Instead of giving them the same quality and nearly the same quantity of provisions that the troops on duty receive, I would give them, as near possible, the same quantity and quality of provisions that the fiendish rebels give our men; and instead of a constant issue of clothing to them, I would let them wear their rags," the officer concluded.

When Assistant Surgeon Gen. A.M. Clark inspected the prison in 1864, he found the prisoners were exceptionally clean, but said the clothing supply was insufficient. Prisoners were allowed to wear clothing sent by relatives, and the government issued clothing almost daily when it was available. Col. Johnson also proclaimed that hundreds of dollars were spent each month to furnish tobacco to the prisoners.

Recollections of the men confined there, published after their release, sharply contrasted with the Union's declaration of humane treatment. B.M. Hord of Nashville, writing in the magazine "Confederate Veteran" in August, 1904, depicted horror and brutality, but it should be remembered this was written 40 years after Hord was confined there. He said:

"Every devilish device that could be conjured up in the brain of a savage to make us suffer was put in force by Johnson. Men were brutally punished on the slightest pretext. I saw prisoners tied up to the fence by their thumbs, their toes barely touching the ground, in the hot broiling sun until they would faint.

"When cut down by the guards, they would fall limp and unconscious, while none of us dared ap-

◀

Gen. Winfield Scott, Commander of United States troops in the Black Hawk Wars, with headquarters on the island of Rock Island.

proach, for they were next to the fence, over the 'dead line' (a ditch prisoners could not approach without being shot without challenge) and grinning sentinels stood just above them with ready guns in hand.''

Hord told how after President Lincoln issued an amnesty proclamation, the U.S. Government opened a "recruiting office" right in the prison. Any Confederate who would swear allegiance to the United States could be sworn into the Union Army with the promise that he'd never have to fight against the South. About 3,000 confederates did defect to the North while they were prisoners at the Arsenal. Those who remained true to the Confederacy denounced the turncoats as "Galvanized Yankees."

Hord related that the soldiers who accepted the

Union offer were moved into new quarters and given preferential treatment, but said rations for the prisoners were reduced and many died of starvation. He said prisoners ate rats, and even a dog they managed to lure into the compound. However, Col. Johnson's official reports to his superiors belied such treatment and indicated the orders for maintaining humane conditions were being carried out to the letter.

To counteract the Union recruiting, the prisoners formed their own camp organization "The Seven Confederate Knights," with their own secret handclasps, signs, password and badge, a seven-pointed star made of shell. They reenlisted all prisoners they could into the military service of the South, forming them into companies of 130 men each under officers.

At one time the prisoners even planned to storm the parapets of their prison with stones, sticks and kitchen knives, overpowering the guards and escaping en masse. But someone tipped Union officers and the guard was doubled. The escape plan was reluctantly abandoned, though records show there were 41 individual escapes from the Arsenal prison. Some escapees were aided by Southern sympathizers in Davenport.

One prisoner, Lafayette Rogan, kept a diary of his experiences, a book still found in the Arsenal's John M. Browning Museum. Rogan had been chosen to serve as recorder for the prison, but he was confined only to the limits of the island and lived outside the stockade. He did not dwell in his diary on ill treatment of prisoners, except to mention the usual hardships of imprisoned men, though he did say there was a lack of clothing and bedding.

As the end of the war approached, the exchange of prisoners increased — 1,005 in February, 2021 in March, and 424 in May, 1865, the last month. A total of 12,409 had been confined there while the prison was in operation.

Of these, 1,968 would never return home. They had died while under confinement. Today more than 1,100 of them still sleep under white markers in the well-kept Confederate Cemetery on Arsenal Island, but not one trace of the prison camp remains. □

▶

Confederate Cemetery; Rock Island Arsenal.

REMARKABLE ANNIE WITTENMYER

Iowa City Historical Society Collection.

In the midst of the wounded and dying on a Civil War battlefield, Annie Wittenmyer conceived the idea for a home that would be a refuge for the orphans of soldiers.

The remarkable and courageous woman the soldiers called "the Angel of Mercy," knew the horrors of war first hand. She had rushed to the front to care for her brother after he was seriously injured in the Civil War. Aghast at the conditions she found in the field hospitals, Mrs. Wittenmyer stayed on to nurse many back to health.

Tirelessly, and without regard to her own health and safety, she traveled from battlefield to battlefield, hospital to hospital. Always her mission was the same — heal, comfort, and improve conditions. One time she arrived with a wagon loaded with food, clothing and medical supplies just in time to save some soldiers who were slowly freezing and starving to death in a rude tent hospital.

Annie Wittenmyer was everywhere, it seemed, in those grim days. She was aboard the steamboat "City of Memphis" as it made its slow journey up the Mississippi River with 750 sick and wounded soldiers from Sherman's Army at Milliken's Bend. The men were en route to a St. Louis Hospital.

One thing that shocked Mrs. Wittenmyer was the fact that men who were terribly ill were being fed the same fare as the other soldiers. She argued, quite effectively, that special diet kitchens should be set up. This was one of her most unique contributions to nursing and established a pattern still in use today. By the close of the war, more than 100 such kitchens had been established.

These photos of the children Anne Wittenmyer cared for are from tintypes of the Civil War period or shortly thereafter. (Iowa City Historical Society Collection.)

One thing that most impressed her as she moved among the wounded and dying was that so often even desperately ill men begged, "Please don't worry about us. See that our families are taken care of."

The soldiers were well aware it was the practice at that time to commit the indigent, including children, to poorhouses. Such unfortunates could even be put out in wholesale lots of work for anyone who would pay for their keep. Many soldiers felt such a fate would befall their families.

Who was this woman, who cared so much for the welfare of others, who chose to expose herself to the disease and dangers of the battlefields? She was born in Sandy Springs, Ohio, on Aug. 20, 1827. In 1847, she married William Wittenmyer, a Jacksonville, Ohio, merchant. She was no stranger to tragedy; of her five children, only one had survived infancy.

The concern of the soldiers for their families touched Mrs. Wittenmyer deeply. When she returned to Iowa, she traveled throughout the state, telling of her war experiences and urging the establishment of a home for soldiers' orphans.

Representatives from many parts of the state met in Muscatine on Oct. 5, 1863, and passed a resolution that an asylum for these children should be established. Annie Wittenmyer was named a member of the board of the organization that evolved from that meeting.

In July, 1864, 21 children were moved into a large brick building in Van Buren County, Iowa. Later, another home was opened at Cedar Falls. Indomitable Annie Wittenmyer was determined that better quarters should be provided, and in 1865, she led a delegation to Washington, D.C. There, using all her considerable persuasiveness, she convinced the Secretary of War that the Army should turn over to her group the relatively new barracks at Camp Kingsman in Davenport. The barracks had not been used since the war.

It was a proud day for Annie Wittenmyer when, on Nov. 16, 1864, the steamer Keithsburg arrived from Keokuk with 150 soldiers' orphans aboard. The Davenport institution was called the "Iowa Soldiers' Orphans' Home" until 1949 when the Iowa legislature changed the name to the "Iowa Annie Wittenmyer Home" to honor its founder.

When the home was opened, Annie Wittenmyer stayed on as matron. Eventually the original concept of the institution changed, and its doors were opened to any neglected child needing loving care and a home. The state assumed control of the Home as a tax-supported institution in 1866.

Annie Wittenmyer felt her job there was done, but she moved on to excel in other fields as author, temperance leader and humanitarian. When she died on Feb. 2, 1900, Annie Wittenmyer left behind many lasting testimonials of a truly remarkable woman. □

LANSING'S LAST RUN

Standing in the pilot house of the steamboat "Lansing" as she chugged upriver on May 13, 1867, Capt. H.M. Hughes squinted at dark clouds on the horizon and remarked to a mate that it appeared a storm might be brewing.

He hoped it wouldn't delay him because everything had gone quite smoothly on this trip and the Lansing was right on schedule. They'd left the Davenport levee right at 8:30 a.m. and should be pulling into Port Byron, Ill., a few miles upstream, in time to make connections with the Western Union Railroad.

The Lansing had gone only a few miles, though, when it encountered strong winds. By the time the craft reached the small landing near Hampton, Ill., the winds were so powerful the steamboat was pinned against the shore. Passengers and crewmen grabbed long poles and pushed hard against the bank, hoping to move the Lansing into deeper water.

It was soon evident to Capt. Hughes that every available bit of power would be needed to do the job, and he ordered resin to be added to the boiler fires to make them hotter. The big paddlewheels were thrown into reverse as the boat attempted to back out.

Up and up went the boiler pressure. The engineer finally hung a three-pound wrench on the safety valve, a dangerous maneuver, but it would allow more pressure to build up. The Lansing shuddered as she struggled to wrest free. And the pressure in the boilers continued to climb upward.

◀

Mississippi River traffic was tremendous in the last century, everything from people to goats was carried by steamboats. Several rivers which are today unnavigable once carried steamboat traffic. (Buffalo Bill Museum Collection.)

When a heavy, thumping sound suddenly rumbled through the boat, Capt. Hughes immediately was aware the thing most feared by rivermen had occurred. The sharp hissing of steam confirmed what he already knew — that the twin boilers had burst under the tremendous pressure. Immediately there was a thundering explosion that sent twisted pieces of metal and a deluge of dust, sand, sticks and rubbish shooting through the boat. Live steam engulfed passengers in the main cabin and their screams were lost in the noise of the walls collapsing around them.

The Hon. Sidney A. Hubbell of Davenport, U.S. district court judge, was sitting in the cabin directly over the rear portion of the boilers when the blast abruptly hurled him 20 feet through one of the aft cabin windows. His foot caught in a window frame. and there he hung, head downward, until he was later freed.

Sitting directly over the boilers, John Kreedler of Clinton was blown clear out of the boat, flying 400 feet in a cloud of steam and red-hot boiler plate. Miraculously, he landed on shore, relatively unscathed. Five other persons nearby were not so lucky. The blast literally tore them apart.

George White of LeClaire had filled in as pilot for an ailing brother-in-law, Robert Allen. White's body was hurled ashore, and when they found it later, three spokes from the wheel had been driven completely through his thighs and his back was broken. Never found was the body of H. Curtis of Davenport, who had been writing a letter when the boilers blew. Five other passengers were so badly injured they never recovered.

An inquest was held into the disaster, and several passengers told of seeing the engineer tie down the safety valve. They said pressure in the boilers had risen from the specified safe limits of 135 pounds to as high as 155 pounds. While the engineer admitted this, he denied that safe limits had been exceeded. He said while the boilers were old, and possibly had been strained, he did not feel they had been particularly unsafe.

One explanation for the explosion, presented at the inquest, was that while the wheel had been working in reverse, it had caused large amounts of mud and sand to be drawn into the boilers, thus blocking some of the pipes.

The once-proud Lansing, first ship built by the famous Diamond Jo Reynolds Line, was completely wrecked. Never again did she sail the Mississippi, boastfully displaying the big diamond emblems, each emblazoned in the center with "Jo," the owner's name. ☐

THE BIG RIVER FLOODS OF LONG, LONG AGO

Every river town along the Mississippi lived in fear of high water. Here Clinton, Iowa residents at the turn of the century make the best of it with a canoe ride up Main Street, while the not-so-venturesome stay high and dry on the boardwalks. (Iowa City Historical Society Collection.)

At most times, the Mississippi is a placid river slowly meandering to the sea. But it also has a dark, demonic face of uncontrolled rage when it embarks on one of its occasional destructive rampages.

No doubt it has been overflowing its banks throughout its history, but the first unusual rise of which we have any account occurred in 1542. De Soto and his followers were at an Indian village on the west side of the river in March of that year, apparently near what is now Helena, Arkansas. They witnessed a rise in the river that covered all of the surrounding countryside for as far as they could see.

The early Spaniards gave to the great river a different name than the Indians. They called it "Rio Grande."

The Indian village that hosted De Soto was on high ground, but even so, the water there reportedly was five to six feet deep. The river remained at that height for several days and then gradually subsided.

The earliest authentic account of a Mississippi area being submerged in flood is of one that occurred in 1724. It is mentioned in "Gould's History of River Navigation," published in the 1880s.

In the archives at Kaskaskia, Ill., is a petition to the crown of France in 1725, for a grant of land in which the damage sustained the year before is mentioned. The villagers were driven to the bluffs on the opposite side of the Kaskaskia River. Their gardens and crops were destroyed and their buildings and property heavily damaged. There is no mention of the height the water reached, but the petition notes that the whole "American Bottom" was submerged.

Old French residents long had a tradition that there was an extraordinary rise in the river between 1740 and 1750, but written accounts of that flooding cannot be found. However, about 1770 the river made further encroachments of the lower and upper stream.

Following what seems to be a cycle of breaking out of its banks, the Mississippi next flooded in 1785, submerging Kaskaskia and Cahokia and large portions of the American Bottom. Though there is only meager information about this great inundation, it is known in the annals of western history as the year of "the Great Waters."

In 1844, soldiers at old Fort Armstrong at Rock Island, Illinois, contended that the Mississippi rose even higher than it had in the great flood of 1785. Certainly, it was deeper at Kaskaskia, where records show it was two feet and five inches above the 1785 mark.

During a gigantic flood in 1811, the river began to rise at St. Louis early in May, and by the 15th had spread over a large portion of the bottoms. It continued to rise for almost a month before it finally hit its peak and began to subside.

During that time, inhabitants of a village below Dubuque, Iowa appealed to their priest to "pray away the water." It is said he gave no encouragement to the people until the river ceased to rise. Then he proposed that they drive off the water by saying masses. As they did this, the water fell rapidly, the ground was soon dry, and a fine crop of corn was raised, which was divided with the priest for saying the masses.

The flood of 1811 exceeded all others recorded until 1823 when the Mississippi covered all of the lands around the upper river and drove people to seek refuge on the bluffs.

Another flood in 1858 almost equalled the height of the waters in 1844. The Ohio River was very high at the same time and there was great destruction of property. Cairo, Illinois, and many other towns in the valley were inundated as levees broke and banks caved in.

High river levels and serious flooding were recorded in 1863, 1867, 1871 and 1875. Great losses occurred in Arkansas, Mississippi and Louisiana when the combined waters of several rivers hit those areas simultaneously. □

Davenport, Rock Island, and Moline all were subject to floods. Here and on the following pages are some of the many disasters that occurred between 1868 and the present. (Putnam Museum Collection.)

THE GREAT ICE GORGE OF 1868

Watching the ice go out of the Mississippi was an awesome spectacle at any time, but on a gray, cold Sunday on March 8, 1868, there were early indications that it was going to be an even bigger show than usual. Residents of Davenport, Iowa, and Rock Island, Illinois, on the other side of the broad river, gathered along their respective levees as the Mississippi smashed its winter chains.

Cold as the day was, it was still warm enough to start the breakup of the heavy ice cover that had capped the river for months. Excited viewers nudged each other and exclaimed at the size of the immense slabs the swollen river was disgorging along both banks. Hourly, the piles grew higher. While the angry waters swirled below, the wildly stacked slabs grew so high that watchers climbed to the very top of them to see the tumultuous drama unfolding in the river.

Yet, almost unnoticed, a small ice gorge was quietly forming at a bend in the river just below Rock Island. With every chunk of ice slammed into it, though, it grew larger. By midnight a cold jagged mass was choking the channel.

The crowds stayed late into the night, warming themselves around bonfires as they waited for the final act when the ice would finally burst loose and go racing downstream in an unstoppable mass. The river was rising rapidly, but few were concerned about it. The growing mountains of ice claimed their full attention. The ice was still sluggish at midnight, the big break had not come, and most of the chilled watchers gave up and went home.

When they awoke the following morning, the levee was flooded, the floe was halted, and the ice gorge downstream was nearly complete. Upstream in the choked channel, an empty log boat that had been lodged above the railroad bridge floated down with an immense escort of ice. En route, it smashed into the draw, which bridge tenders vainly tried to swing out of the way. The boat snaked its way downstream, finally wedging in a field of ice between the two cities.

That morning five men climbed over the frozen ice hill on the Davenport levee and picked their way across the floe in a daring attempt to save the wrecked boat. But as they got on its deck, the ice began moving on either side. From both shores came screams of "Get off! Hurry! It's going!"

The men scrambled off. One of them fell in the swirling waters, but was saved by a brave man in a rowboat. Caught in a cluster of ice, the damaged log boat moved downstream. Very soon, overwhelmed by massive chunks of ice, it sank. The men had departed just in time.

By 10 a.m. of that day a broad tract of unbroken ice in the middle of the river struck the head of Turner's Island, stopping the whole floating mess once again. Like a cork in a bottle, the jam dammed up the boiling waters behind it. The river rose with frightening speed.

In less than 30 minutes, the riverfront was deserted and flooded. Homes were hastily abandoned to the fast-rising waters; their owners carried what they could to higher ground and came back for more in small skiffs that soon floated up to second-story windows.

Rats, flushed from winter quarters, headed for the bluffs in droves. With them went frightened Davenporters. By noon, Davenport's Front Street was one long stretch of murky water and giant floating ice slabs. Cellars and basements were full. And still the waters rose higher.

In the basement kitchen of the Scott House, girls left half-prepared dinners on the stoves as the river began pouring through windows and doors. When they returned later, they found soggy loaves of bread still sitting in the ovens.

Davenport's ferry dock was forced from its moorings and shoved downstream for several blocks. A small bridge to a mill was swept away. In Rock Island, mammoth piles of ice jammed against the wagon bridge from Arsenal Island to the mainland, sweeping the entire span away. Even the sturdily-built railroad bridge suffered severe damage as ice piled high against its creaking timbers.

Just up-river in Moline, Illinois, a break in a dam allowed water to pour through to several manufacturing plants, damaging Deere & Co. and many other firms. By late Monday, the ice had piled so high between Davenport and Rock Island that residents could not see each others' cities, except from second or third-story windows.

Front Street, all the way from East Davenport to the City Cemetery, a distance of several miles, had become an ice-clogged river. Floating with the ice cakes were household furnishings, chicken houses, lumber and hundreds of other items.

Fast-moving chunks of ice rammed into sides of buildings, ripping off corners. Wooden sidewalks were uprooted and heavy posts smashed like matchsticks. In the midst of the maelstrom, Claussen's Lime House caught fire, but firemen couldn't reach it because of the water. Davenport's Flat Iron Square became a battered wreck.

By 9 p.m. that evening, the ice field extended for a full 100 miles above the Quad-Cities. The pressure of water behind it kept the ice sweeping down with tremendous force.

Finally, even the gargantuan dam of ice could no longer resist the build-up behind it. With a roar reportedly heard 30 miles away, the gorge weakened and let go. Within a half-hour, the water in the Quad-Cities had receded several feet, and by midnight, the river was back in its banks.

Cleanup operations continued for weeks. There were no official estimates of damages, but it was generally agreed that they exceeded a million dollars, a huge sum for those times.

There have been other ice jams on the Mississippi, including some impressive ones in recent years, but nothing in the memory of man has equalled the terrible gorge of 1868. □

ROUGH AND READY RAFTSMEN

They were as ornery as the currents in the big river they worked, and as tough as the logs on which they risked their lives. They were the brawling, intrepid raftsmen who pushed and shoved and guided great floating masses of logs down the Mississippi River to the sawmills.

It was no job for the faint-hearted, or for the clumsy, because a raftsman, above all, had to be sure-footed as he scampered across the floating, ever-treacherous logs.

Buffalo Bill Museum Collection.

One couplet of the day paid this tribute to the raftsman's toughness:

"He never shaved the whiskers
From off his horny hide;
He drove them in with hammers
And chawed them off inside."

Down the river from the pine country, the raftsmen came to Quad-City lumber mills. They lived in lean-tos or rude tents pitched right on the rafts, and it's said, spent most of their working days falling into the river, wrestling logs and each other, and calling to the girls on shore.

Some raftsmen became legends on the river, rugged men, like "Double-Headed Bob," "Sailor Jack," "Big John," and "Whiskey Jack."

The nicknames raftsmen bore usually referred to some deed or misdeed they'd performed, or to some peculiar facet of their personality.

The logging industry in Minnesota and Wisconsin brought loggers floating downriver to deliver logs to Davenport and Muscatine sawmills. The logical way to deliver logs was to form them into rafts and ride them down river. (Iowa State Historical Society Collection.)

There was one roughneck dubbed, "Silly Jack." He could neither read nor write, and when he signed any document at the sawmill or lumber office, he scribbled a big "X" instead of his name. One day he jotted down an "XX" instead of just plain "X". When a bookkeeper expressed wonder, "Silly Jack" explained he and a saloon lady at Muscatine had just been married and he thought that being a married man, he should change his name.

Life on the rafts was hard, and men were always exposed to the elements. Many raftsmen fell overboard and were never seen again. On most rafts, the men took turns doing the cooking. One man cooked until someone else complained. Then the man who complained had to take his place.

One of these temporary cooks, Jem Wilson, hated the job and vowed to do such a terrible job that he'd be allowed to return to the oars. Accordingly, he made a huge batch of biscuits and dumped in enough salt for an army.

One man took a bite of biscuit and shouted, "Great guns, these biscuits are pure salt!" But then, realizing a complaint would make him the next cook, he quickly added, "They're the best I ever did eat!"

Once a raft was launched, it went on night and day until it was steered to its destination. This often involved a trip of several hundred miles. If the river was straight, the night watch had little to do, and the steersman had trouble staying awake. For that reason he always held a big wrench in his hand. If he dozed, the clang would certainly awake him, or someone else on the raft.

When they went ashore, raftsmen spent every cent they had, and it wasn't unusual for them to become involved in brawls with townspeople, who resented their free-wheeling ways. Saloon keepers generally welcomed the lavish-spenders, though their establishments were often a shambles after the raftsmen had left.

An old song, still sometimes sung today by folk singers, pays a back-handed compliment to the social graces of raftsmen:

"I see you are a raftsman, sir,
And not a common bum;
For no one but a raftsman
Stirs coffee with his thumb." □

Buffalo Bill Museum Collection.

BURLESQUE IN DAVENPORT

Burtis Opera House in Davenport, Iowa.

Some of the finest theatrical productions in the world were presented in the Midwest in its early days, and speakers of wide renown, even such personages as Mark Twain, trod the boards of opera houses. But there were shocked cries of outrage when May Fisk and her troupe of English blondes appeared upon the stage of the venerable old theaters in the fall of 1878.

"Shocking!" and "Disgraceful" were some of the milder epithets that issued from respectable matrons and the pulpit. This was the Midwest's first (but certainly not last) exposure to burlesque and it was a long time before the shock waves finally died down.

The performance was somewhat suggestively billed as May Fisk and her grand collection of naughty girls, and they played to packed houses, who shelled out the equivalent of two days' wages to see the blonde imports traipse across the stage.

Many church groups had sought to prevent the show from being held, and some even appeared to protest in a delegation before the city councils, but the show went on anyway. In fact, one newspaper noted wryly that "every Sunday School in town was represented in the theater the night of the performance."

The newspaper's review was rather lukewarm: "The entertainment itself was of the simplest rag-tag type, but it was not a bad show. Many of the illusions, dances and skits bordered on vulgarity, but this could be expected for this was a burlesque company."

"The beauty — such as it was — was in the form of blondes. They were of the fairest hair, and very saucy. Madame Senyeah's stunt on the rolling globe was most unusual, and it is fortunate there was not a lady in the house, for the Ninepin dance (Europe's latest sensation) ending the show, was naughty."

In Keokuk, Iowa, May Fisk and her troupe were refused a license to perform by the mayor. This prompted the Davenport Democrat to observe snidely that, "That proper town of Keokuk is now safe."

During the next ten years, assorted burlesque acts continued to appear though they could always be counted upon to stir some protest. But there were also fine dramatic productions like "East Lynne," and "Jane Eyre."

There were other forms of entertainment for Midwesterners in those days, too, magic shows, mindreading and spiritualistic acts, and many lectures on serious and humorous subjects. One time a monster whale 60 feet long and originally weighing 80,000 pounds, went on display for the admission price of just five cents.

At one time, crowds jammed theaters to see Dr. Charles Slade, ballyhooed as "the far-famed and celebrated spirit medium from New York."

The good doctor promised his audiences to "demonstrate spirit power in full gas light." Whether or not he succeeded, his crowd apparently enjoyed the show, and the ticket office cash registers jingled merrily. ☐

'BANISH THE BRUTE'

This early steam car, although not in Davenport, is typical of the type they called "the brute."

"The Brute" was just one of the uncomplimentary names Davenporters called the first motorized street car to appear in the city. Other incensed citizens loudly protested it was "an abomination," "a pox on the city," and "an insult to old Dobbin." And, there were those who sniffed delicately and proclaimed it "a smelly monster."

The officials of the People's Railway Co. were taken aback because they'd never dreamed of such an adverse public reaction when they'd introduced the big, steam-driven street car in 1878. True, they'd retired Dobbin without much advance notice, and the citizens, at least some of them, vehemently resisted the sudden change.

For many years street cars had been hauled up steep Brady Street Hill by straining horses. Teams were stationed at both the top and bottom of the hill to relieve the working horses. Many people had declared the horses had to perform inhumane tasks and demanded that the railway company do something about it. And when they did — they complained.

Some dubbed the new-fangled contraption "The Brady Street Brute," or the "Hill Monster," or more simply "The Motor." The Democrat newspaper commented critically: "It is very doubtful whether we are large enough as a city to even allow power to be used on any of our city street railroads. Certainly the necessity for such steam power is not now apparent and in no event should one of the leading streets of the city be condemned for such a purpose."

It seemed no one had a good word for the streetcar. Critics said it was worse than having a steam engine chugging through the streets. It was true the "Brute" wasn't beautiful by any standards.

It was nine feet long, 12 feet high and weighed 12,000 pounds. From its towering stack belched black smoke. A squat boiler gave it a duck-waddling appearance. Painted on the front and sides in bright yellow letters was "No. 1, People's Tramway, Brady Street, Davenport, Iowa."

The "Brute" served much as a railroad locomotive, pushing cars on tracks from 5th Street to the top of Brady Hill and towing them back down again. True, no one could deny the streetcar was faster. It made it up the hill in just three minutes. The sweating horses had required at least 10 minutes. Horses reared and bolted in horror when they approached the smoking monster. A number of minor accidents occurred as a result of this.

The smoke and noise fostered constant complaints from citizens, who said it sounded like elephants dancing on kettle drums when the "Brute" strained up the hill.

One woman, in a letter to the editor published in the Democrat, declared residents along Brady Street were suffering lung diseases from breathing the "Brute's" noxious fumes. One citizen warned that people would "take matters into their own hands" if the streetcar wasn't abolished.

Though abashed by this reception, railway officials had sunk $2,700 in the streetcar and could not be dissuaded to abandon it. Besides, it obviously operated more quickly and efficiently than had the horses.

In an ad they proclaimed, "Cars can travel faster and make quicker trips. We cannot turn our backs to a progressive measure. That it will prove to be a popular thing can hardly be doubted."

In a conciliatory move, railway officials replaced coal with coke to cut down somewhat on the smoke and noxious odors the "Brute" gave off. Eventually the protests dwindled away and the scoffers finally accepted it as a necessary evil. The street car chugged on and on until it was eventually replaced by the electric trolley. □

'HERE COMES THE CIRCUS!'

Early settlers didn't lack for entertainment. It was considered a real musical treat to pay $1.50 for a reserved seat to hear Ole Bull, the concert violinist. The popular theater attractions included Susan Denin's appearance in "Lady of Lyons." There were other such offerings as "Seven Girls in Uniform," a two-act operetta presented entirely in German.

Something that awed early audiences was billed as an "aerial steamship." Its promoters claimed it could "ascend to any altitude under aerostatic power at the will of the machinist (pilot)."

The strange-looking device was propelled by steam, and if audiences never did witness any attempt to lift it off the ground, they still paid their money just to look at it.

Big crowds lined levees to watch the arrival of the first showboat that chugged upriver from New Orleans and St. Louis. Far and away the most popular of these was the "Banjo," and long before its arrival big billboards always proclaimed "The Banjo is Coming." It offered mirth, music, and a seating capacity for 800.

Typical circus parade of the 1890's. (Redhead Collection, Bentonsport, Iowa.)

Popular, too, with the early settlers were the many quite posh emporiums that dispensed beer and German music. One of the most patronized was Herr Weidmann's Davenport Gardens atop the Ripley Street bluffs. This is how an early writer described a typical night there:

"The place was thronged by 1,500 persons, male and female. Everyone enjoyed themselves, judging from the jumbled crowd as it swayed and rolled around the room. Cask after cask of beer was tapped and drained."

Right behind the pioneers who settled the Mississippi Valley came that most venturesome form of entertainment, the circus, wagons rumbling through hub-deep mud, over hills and across streams, to reach and delight the inhabitants of the frontier settlements.

And what wonders they brought with them! White men and Indians jostled one another in their eagerness to be first inside the tents. When George Bailey's circus arrived, the settlers gaped at animals most had never seen before — elephants, giraffes — even a huge hippopotamus billed as "the cataclysm of all wonders." But it was the elephant, with a "tail at either end" that really intrigued the Indians.

Herr Driesbach's circus featured "a magnificent living giraffe", and "the largest and most famous performing elephant in the world."

Not only did circuses find their way to the isolated little settlements between 1855-'65, but there were the gaudy, wonderful showboats, touring theatrical groups, operettas, piano concerts—and even Swiss bellringers. For a half dollar one could enjoy the best seat in most theaters.

There was even a form of "motion pictures," or at least the forerunner of them, the "panorama," which was painted scenery parading across the stage in an endless roll. Sellout crowds viewed Risley's "Grand colossal moving panorama of the River Thames."

At least one circus, and often two, found its way to the settlements each summer. The circuses followed a regular circuit, stopping first at Port Byron, moving then to Rock Island, across to Davenport by ferry, since there was no bridge across the Mississippi River in the early days, and then on downriver to Muscatine.

The arrival of the circus was always a gala occasion and the town assumed a holiday air as soon as the first wagons rolled into its streets. Traditionally, Antonio Bros.' circus always arrived at midmorning, led by a team of high-stepping Arabian horses and a colorfully outfitted cornet band.

One of the features of North's National Circus was a foot race held after each performance. Customers were invited to take part in a race through downtown streets, the winner to receive a silver goblet said to be "easily worth $30." Main circus acts were generally gladiators, tumblers, and singing minstrels, for the day of the big circuses was still just around the corner. □

———————————————————————— ∎

CIRCUS BROUGHT ELECTRICITY

Today we take for granted the fact we can flip a switch and flood a room with light, but when Midwesterners got their first glimpse of the properties of electricity in 1880, they considered it nothing short of a miracle. It's strange, too, that this marvel arrived, not shepherded by a group of scientists, but aboard a swaying, creaking circus wagon.

In a way, this was the proper entry, for electricity at that time was still considered something of a novelty, a thing rightfully aligned with carnival ballyhoo and sideshows. It was the traveling Great London Circus that brought the wonders of the future to frontier towns.

It could be expected that advertisements proclaiming the magical properties of electricity might be quite "circusy," and, indeed, they were.

"Heaven's own gift to earth! Ethereal rays shedding a halo of imperishable glory over all surrounding objects! It fairly glows with phosphorescent ef-

Circus wagon typical of the kind used during the last century. (Iowa State Historical Society Collection.)

fulgence! Turns the darkest, densest, blackest night into glorious sunlit day! It is like the rays of a dozen dazzling suns concentrated!" So boasted the posters.

The electrically-operated lights demonstrated by the circus were of the carbon arc type. One of the show's features was a 35-horsepower engine that operated the electricity-producing machine. In a news story of the event, a newspaper reported the circus offered "the bright glare of 12 lamps that lit up the night with the softness of mid-day. One light is equal to 3,000 candle power, or nearly 200 gas lights, and is cheaper by 75 percent than gas or coal oil."

The circus demonstration gave people a glimpse into the future, and within the next few years arc light installation became commercially feasible. And about this time, newspapers began to carry accounts of a young inventor named Thomas A. Edison who had, it was said, "perfected a filament in a vacuum bulb which, when electricity is passed through, glows brighter than several gas jets."

It was further explained that the new Edison light "has no flame, soot, smell or grime. It should spell the end of the oil lamp and looks to be better than gas. No more wicks to trim, no chimneys to clean, no oily lamps to fill." There were even some far-sighted souls who predicted that by the far-off date of 1939, electric lights would be in general use, even on city streets.

Said one forecaster who didn't set his sights high enough, "Citizens out of an evening without horse and rig probably will feel safer with these electric lights on the street!" Lights were a big feature in 1881 at a ball sponsored by the Davenport Turner Society.

In May, 1882, the Brush Electric Light Co. was organized in the area, and in November, Merchants' Electric Light Co. of Moline went into operation. The same year, Davenport Electric Light Co. came into being. To Rock Island goes the honor of having completed its electric light firm first. Its facilities included 11 towers, each 125 feet high, equipped with arc lights that spread a soft glow over the downtown area.

From each tower were suspended two light units, making a total of 22 units, for which Rock Island paid $365 per light per year. In 1883, a 20-light dynamo was installed in Davenport's old gas plant, the present site of the French & Hecht Co. Becoming more and more modern, Davenport two years later ordered installation of 35 tower lights and 45 lamps at street intersections. Moline during 1884 installed a 50-light electric arc machine for its citizens. By the mid 1880's, the Midwest was emerging from the darkness. Edison's new light, reaching perfection, would make life even brighter. □

HE SAWED THEIR HORNS

Only a brute, a callous, inhuman fiend, would be cruel enough to saw the horns off his cattle. And on that hot summer day in 1885, farmers and towns-people in Geneseo, Ill., crowded into Squire Steele's little courtroom just to see Herman H. Haaff receive his proper punishment.

The farmers present muttered threateningly as Haaff entered the room. They whispered to one another that cutting off a cow's horns was like yanking a human's hair or fingernails out by the roots. It was a shocking, unthinkable thing to do, and a man who would do that deserved anything he got.

The people of Geneseo were really surprised that Haaff would perform such an inhumane act. They knew him as a very good farmer who had 4,000

acres of lush land just north of Atkinson, Ill., in Henry County. He was considered a bit eccentric, but no one had thought him cruel.

People said it all started when Haaff got mad at his big bull after the animal tried to attack him. They said Haaff had vowed to show the bull who was boss, and had forced the animal's head into a stanchion, and quickly sawed off its horns.

Haaff really expected the animal to fall into a stupor after such an operation, but it showed absolutely no ill effects. If anything, it was a much better humored beast afterward. Horns on cattle were a nuisance, Haaff reasoned, and if it had worked so well on the bull, why not dehorn all his cattle?

People said he'd rounded up all his cattle, shoved their heads into stanchions, and sawed away until he had a pile of horns like a winter's wood supply. But neighbors spied Haaff's dehorned cattle and passed the word, and horrified letters and telegrams began to pour into the headquarters of the Illinois Humane Society. Newspapers blazoned the story of Farmer Haaff, the torturer of dumb animals.

In no time, representatives of the Humane Society were in Geneseo to see for themselves. One look and they had Haaff hauled before Squire Steele. The trial continued for three days in a packed courtroom.

Haaff was no simple man who would willingly let himself be convicted of a charge he considered entirely unjust. He produced witness after witness who testified that the cattle seemed to feel no pain whatever, and began to eat again as soon as their horns were lopped off.

As similar testimony unfolded, farmers in the courtroom began to look questioningly at one another. They all knew well no animal that was sick or in pain would eat. Was it possible dehorning didn't hurt, after all?

In no time, the crowd that had been so hostile went over to Haaff. Newspapers, taking their cue, began advocating that all horns come off. Hadn't many people been injured by horns, some fatally? And when you stopped to think of it, why should cattle have horns in the first place?

The agent of the Humane Society wasn't so easily convinced. Granted that cutting off the horns didn't hurt anymore than removing a human fingernail, God had placed the horns on the cattle. Therefore it was wicked for men to remove them.

Lawyers for Haaff argued that horns were once necessary for cattle to protect themselves and their young from wolves. But the wolves were long gone and the horns were no longer needed, so it only followed they must go, too.

Those in the courtroom cheered loudly and the Humane Society agent hung his head and kept his silence. In a short time the dehorning of cattle became so commonplace there were men who made it their profession. It was noted by farmers that dehorned cattle were more comfortable, safer, couldn't gore one another, and even required less feed.

Eventually selective and cross-breeding produced cattle without horns. Few today even remember Herman Haaff and the great de-horning controversy.

□

BEWARE THE 'KISSING BUG'

If it really were a hoax, as many believed, then the strange, and sometimes hilarious, saga of the "kissing bug" fooled and terrified a lot of people in the Mississippi Valley, as well as other parts of the nation.

Nobody had ever heard of a "kissing bug" until the summer of 1899, when alleged victims of its deadly bites began exhibiting all sorts of strange symptoms, and there were many who said they had spotted and even done battle with them.

It was said the "kissing bug" appropriately chose the victim's lips as its target, zooming in, implanting a peck or bite, and then winging off after the next victim. And the stories they told about that pesky bug!

Everyone had heard about the farmer who was attacked by a "kissing bug" and drove his team at breakneck speed for five miles just to get home and get in his house before it got him.

Then there was the farmhand who said he'd been bitten while milking a cow, and before he could even get into the house, his lip had swollen so much it weighed four pounds. If anyone asked how he managed to weigh his lip, it isn't recorded. People took the "kissing bug" attack quite seriously and newspapers reported an epidemic sweeping the nation.

For example, there was a warning in the July 15, 1899, edition of the Davenport Democrat, stating "the bug is headed this way," and describing its antics in other areas. A Des Moines paper reported the bug had reached the city and commented, "It may be expected from now on that many of the women of the city will be out with a net after dark trying to capture one of the osculating creatures."

In line with keeping its readers well informed, the Democrat solemnly warned, "The kissing bug is no joke. Several hundred people here now realize this, and noting its arrival in this country, are awaiting its appearance with eager anticipation. They fear the worst. We are not safe here. They have it plenty in Chicago. It is coming our way. It may appear here at any moment. There'll be trouble when it does come."

It seems probable the newspapers viewed the bug with tongue-in-cheek, but people walked around ready to clap a hand over their lips at the first suggestion of a buzz or whir. And then, two days after the warning article in the Democrat, the first "kissing bug" attack was reported in Moline, Ill. A young girl awoke in the morning to find her lip greatly swollen. The attending physician expressed doubts, but conceded that "the bug" could have been the culprit. In short order, five more cases were reported in Scott County.

Each tale of an attack bordered on the improbable, but the most fantastic of all was duly recorded in a blow-by-blow account in the Democrat. It involved a Davenport father who rushed to his daughter's aid when he heard her screaming in a nearby room. There the father found the girl's suitor, bravely doing his best to fight off an invading "kissing bug."

Said the Democrat, "The father tried to land a right hook on the bug, but the bug deftly sidestepped and jabbed him in the jaw. Shortly, the father landed in the geranium bed, and the bug got mad." The account described the insect as "terribly enraged and its eyes showed with a green light while its stinger vibrated like a jigsaw and made an alarming humming sound, interspersed with screeches like a bat's.

"It gnashed its fangs all the while and foam dripped from its red lips and its forked tongue played in and out of its mouth like lightning."

Not one to take abuse from a mere insect, the father, according to the account, picked up a shotgun and stalked his prey.

"His first shot cut the clothesline and let a week's washing into the dirt. The second hit the dog of a neighbor with whom he had not been sociable for over a year. Then he clubbed his gun and fought at close quarters. He caught the bug a crack with the butt end of the weapon and knocked it out."

Apparently the "kissing bug" was made of stern stuff, for it reportedly revived and escaped. The man who had been courageously trying to protect his daughter was less lucky. He was hauled into court on charges of disturbing the peace and discharging firearms within the city limits.

As proof that the bug wasn't invincible, Davenport City Clerk Al J. Smith killed what he purported to be one, and displayed it at city hall. Several merchants offered to buy it to display in their windows.

The "kissing bug" was described as "nearly an inch in length, black, with a proboscis and the identical and unmistakable shape that appears in likenesses of him that have been so plentiful in the papers of late."

To those who scoffed, believers in the "kissing bug" pointed to no less an authority than Webster's Dictionary, which identified such an insect as "Melanolestes Picipes, any of several species of bloodsucking, venomous Hemiptera that sometimes bite the lip, or other parts of the human body, causing painful sores."

Whatever it was, or if it was at all, the "kissing bug" disappeared after a few sorties and was never seen again. □

'BUFFALO BILL' CODY

Iowa's contribution to the lore and legends of the Wild West was a major one, for it gave the country and the world the most colorful character of them all — William (Buffalo Bill) Cody.

Into one lifetime "Buffalo Bill" piled up triumphs in successive careers as scout, Indian fighter, buffalo hunter and world-renowned showman. Today, years after his death, there's scarcely a youngster who hasn't heard of the exploits and adventures of dashing "Buffalo Bill." His name and fame are commem-

orated in such places as the Cody Museum in Cody, Wyo., the Buffalo Bill Museum near his birthplace in LeClaire, Iowa, and the restored Cody family home near McCausland, Iowa.

There is no general agreement on the exact location of Cody's birthplace, except that it did occur in Scott County. LeClaire proudly proclaims itself as "The Birthplace of Buffalo Bill," and there is no doubt he spent many of his formative years there.

Some argue that Cody was born on a farm on the banks of the Wapsipinicon River near Princeton, Iowa, while others contend the site was on the Territory Road leading from LeClaire to Argo, about one-and-a-half miles from LeClaire. There are still others who believe "Buffalo Bill," christened William Frederick Cody, was born in a log cabin on Glynn's Creek in Butler township, several miles north of LeClaire.

His father was Isaac Cody, a restless, energetic man who decided to move his family to Kansas after his son, Sammy, was thrown from a wild pony on their Walnut Grove farm and killed. The elder Cody was also intensely interested in the slavery controversy then broiling in Kansas.

LeClaire, Iowa, claims Buffalo Bill Cody as its own. Memorabilia of his life may be seen at the Buffalo Bill Museum at LeClaire.

BUFFALO BILL-WM. F. COL

By 1860, "Buffalo Bill" had begun his career as a pony express rider, carrying the mail from one outpost to another. As a boy, he had sat barefoot under LeClaire, Iowa's famous "Green Tree," watching the Mississippi River flow by and dreaming of adventure. In the West he would find more than he had ever imagined.

The next year, "Buffalo Bill" signed up with the rough and tumble Seventh Kansas cavalry, remaining with the group until 1865. He won the name he would carry to his grave in 1867 for the feat of killing 4,280 buffalo in 18 months under a contract whereby he was to furnish the Kansas Pacific Railroad with meat for the men constructing the line.

Still, "Buffalo Bill" might have remained an obscure cowboy, but for the imaginative pen of a flamboyant writer named Ned Buntline. When Buntline met "Buffalo Bill," he realized he was a made-to-order hero. Soon youngsters all over America were thrilling to dime novel accounts of the exciting adventures of "Buffalo Bill." Cody fit the picture of a dashing hero with his shoulder-length hair, jutting beard and moustache. Though Buntline often exaggerated his accounts of "Buffalo Bill's" deeds, the former Scott County resident did much to add to his own legend.

From 1868 to 1872, he was a scout in campaigns against the dreaded Sioux and Cheyenne Indians. All of his exploits were colorfully reported by Buntline and others. Always ready for something different, "Buffalo Bill" entered politics in 1872, becoming a member of the Nebraska legislature, a job he soon found too tame for him.

Four years later, he was in the saddle again, this time as scout for the troops and was often in the forefront of major battles against the Indians. He became even more of a legend when he killed a Cheyenne chief in a bloody, hand-to-hand battle. It is said "Buffalo Bill" took part in more campaigns against the Indians than any man living at the time.

Abruptly he embarked upon a new and wholly different career. He became the manager and star attraction of "Buffalo Bill's Wild West Show," and for a quarter of a century toured the United States and Europe, appearing before millions.

No. 351
FEB. 1, 1908
BUFFALO BILL'S FLATBOAT DRIFT
FIVE CENTS
THE BUFFALO BILL STORIES
A Weekly Publi... devoted to Border History
STREET & SMITH, PUBLISHERS, NEW YORK

One of the stars of his show became almost as well known as himself. Under his skilled tutelage, Annie Oakley created an amazing shooting act. She could break glass balls from horseback, clip the ashes from a cigar someone held in his teeth, or snap pennies from between her husband's clenched fingers.

Many times during the early 1900's "Buffalo Bill" brought his Wild West show back to the land of his birth. When the old scout and Indian fighter retired, he devoted his attention to his lands in Wyoming.

"Buffalo Bill" died in 1917, his place in the ranks of America's folk heroes forever secure. □

'CUT DOWN THOSE POLES'

George Washington McCaskrin, Rock Island's mayor in 1906, was a man who did his duty as he saw it, and sometimes took direct action without waiting for the slow-moving wheels of justice to finish turning.

His motto was: "Act now, and let them decide later if it's legal." What he lacked in tact, he more than made up for in direct action — even if it did sometimes embarrass the administration.

There was the time, in January, 1906, that the Union Electric Telephone Co. had erected a number of poles without first obtaining permission from the city. Hizzoner didn't go to the legal department, or send any polite notes pointing out the infraction. Instead, he hauled a number of policemen to the scene, handed them axes, pointed at the poles, and ordered, "chop 'em down!"

The telephone company quickly got the point — no permits, no poles. Mayor McCaskrin's next targets were the powerful railroads. He charged that the DRI & NW and the Burlington and Milwaukee

Davenport, Iowa circa 1920.

Railroad Lines had conspired to defraud Rock Island shippers by charging exorbitant rates. No courts or injunctions for mayor McCaskrin, no waiting for Congress to establish railroad rates.

No sir! At 3:30 p.m. one April day in 1906, the mayor served notice upon the railroads that they had forfeited their right-of-way through the city. He gave astounded railroad officials just five minutes to digest this momentous news before he put a crew to work tearing up tracks in front of the depot.

Protests meant nothing, nor threats of legal action. Once again the "workmen" were police officers, and they were protected by guards armed with shotguns. In short order, the men tore up 30 feet of track and ties. The railroad men countered by switching their trains to the Rock Island-Peoria tracks.

This didn't faze Mayor McCaskrin who was on the scene supervising the track removal. He just moved his men down to the other tracks and ripped up another 30 feet, completely paralyzing all railroad operations in Rock Island. Guards stood by to make certain no repairs were made.

The situation became quite tense, with rival Democrats charging Mayor McCaskrin with "setting the nation on its ear" by holding up the U.S. mail. The powerful railroads reacted quickly and soon obtained court injunctions to prohibit any further damage to the tracks. Repairs were made and the trains began to run again without any more interference from the mayor.

But McCaskrin was satisfied. He felt he'd "seen his duty and done it" as he'd been elected to do. □

MIDWEST NOT IMMUNE TO EARTHQUAKES

Natural disasters like floods, tornadoes and crippling storms were no strangers to Mississippi Valley residents, but on the night of July 18, 1909, when the walls of homes set up a strange trembling and dishes unaccountably rattled in the pantries, there were many who felt certain the world was coming to an end.

It was no wonder Midwesterners were frightened. They were experiencing one of the few earthquakes ever to be recorded in the area's history. The Palimpsest, monthly publication of the Iowa State Historical Society, notes that the quake had its epicenter near Springfield, Ill., and the tremor was felt through much of western Illinois and eastern Iowa.

Though no one was injured, the shock was sufficient to shake down a few chimneys. The tremors awakened people, many of whom ran into the streets looking dazed. Some said pictures swayed on their walls and dishes rattled violently. There was reportedly one hard shock followed by two lesser tremors.

This wasn't the first time earthquakes had been felt in the Mississippi Valley area, though such instances have been quite rare in recorded history. For example, on the evening of Aug. 31, 1886, an earthquake that caused heavy damage in Charleston, S.C., extended its shock waves over an area 1,000 miles in diameter, from Boston to Cuba and from Bermuda to Iowa. The ground trembled in Keokuk, Iowa, and in Burlington occupants of high buildings quickly evacuated. Printers in a Dubuque, Iowa newspaper building "ran for their lives," while an audience in an opera house was "very much frightened," according to the Palimpsest.

About 11 p.m. on Sept. 26, 1891, an earthquake that varied in the intensity of force was felt in part of Iowa. A number of frightened Amana residents felt the ground shaking. Tipton residents reported hearing a rumbling like a freight train passing. A Keokuk, Iowa, doctor said his whole house shook violently.

The most pronounced earthquake in Iowa history shook Keokuk again at 5:30 a.m. on Oct. 31, 1895. This massive earth tremor was felt by residents in 23 states. There were two distinct shocks, each lasting approximately 25 seconds, with a short intermission between. The shock rattled windows and chimneys. E.T. Bartruff said later that several gallons of cream were churned into fine butter on his farm near Moar, Iowa. Walter Brinkman declared the ashes were shaken from his furnace, while B.F. Hagerman insisted the buttons had been rattled off his trousers. Two shocks were recorded in Dubuque, but there was no damage.

On April 13, 1905, another tremor was felt in Keokuk, but there was no serious damage. During the year of 1909, three earthquakes were reported in Iowa and several towns in the eastern part of the state reported feeling the tremors. Dubuque apparently felt the brunt of one of these and the shock was particularly noticeable in higher buildings. Girls in one overall factory fled to the street in terror, while a workman on a 40-foot scaffold became so frightened he jumped, fortunately landing unhurt in a pile of sand. Three very distinct tremors were felt in Dubuque on Jan. 2, 1912. It was sufficient to knock glassware from shelves, but damage was slight. Southeast Iowa was shaken again on April 9, 1917, by a quake that covered an area of 200,000 square miles from Kansas to Ohio, and from Wisconsin to Mississippi.

The shock of this quake was sufficient in Iowa City to shake offices in the Johnson County Bank Building, where desks and tables slid across the floor and books tumbled from shelves. Similar effects were noted in Bellevue, Clinton, Davenport and Muscatine.

Dubuque, which seems to be the most earthquake-prone of Iowa cities, rattled again on March 1, 1925, from a tremor originating in Canada. Tall buildings shook and advertising signs swayed as though a strong wind were blowing.

In the 90 years since the first earthquake was recorded in Iowa, there has been a total of 18 shocks and many milder disturbances. The shocks have ranged from "force readings" of 3 to 8, but no Iowan has ever died in an earthquake in the state, and damage has always been minor.

The reason for Iowa's apparent imperviousness to earthquakes, experts feel, may be the heavy glacial drift that covers almost the entire state and could act as a giant shock absorber for seismic disturbances. □

Drawing by Henry Lewis.

HONOR TO FORT ARMSTRONG

President Woodrow Wilson pushed a button that released 100 white doves, painted Indians skirmished in mock battles, 100 guns boomed a salute, and Quad-Citians spent six fun-filled days celebrating the 100th anniversary of the establishment of Fort Armstrong on the present site of Rock Island Arsenal.

Time was turned back to the days of Chief Black Hawk and old Zachary Taylor during June 18-24, 1916, as the gala festival commemorating the founding of the westernmost frontier fort produced one extravaganza after another.

Third Ave. in Moline, Illinois circa 1910. (A & A Coins, Stamps, and Collectables.)

Led by historians and businessmen, the area turned out en masse to make the anniversary celebration the most extravagant ever staged in the Upper Mississippi Valley up to that time. There were pageants, parades, fireworks and races, historic addresses, special events, and water and land fetes day after day. Nor was the celebration purely local. Hundreds of former residents returned to the Quad-Cities to participate, and it was also homecoming for many Indians.

Descendants of Indians who had once lived in the area came from the federal reservation at Tama, Iowa and erected wickiups on the island. They also took part in sham battles to commemorate those their ancestors had fought with U.S. soldiers. From Kansas came direct descendants of Chief Black Hawk. In the White House in Washington, President Wilson pressed a button which notified a wireless radio station at Arlington, Va. to flash a message to the Arsenal that the celebration was officially under way.

The signal also caused the release of 100 white doves and hundreds of gas-filled balloons. A huge American flag was unfurled, while the wireless operator relayed the President's greetings to Quad-Citians.

On the Sunday preceding the beginning of the celebration many area churches held special commemorative services. Band concerts were held in Fejervary Park and at other recreation sites. In the afternoon, the time trials of the special racing event "the Centennial Derby" were held in Davenport.

At 6:15 a.m. of the opening day, 100 guns on Arsenal Island boomed a salute. The chief event of the day was a pageant depicting the "Coming of the First Flag" to the area in 1805. In conjunction with the event, more than 700 Pioneer Settlers of Scott and Rock Island Counties met on the pageant grounds to relive old times.

Judge James Bollinger delivered an address dedicating the old Arsenal building. A dedicatory address at the pier of the first bridge over the Mississippi River was given by attorney Charles Grilk. J.B. Oakleaf of Moline spoke at the dedication of the old home of Col. Davenport on the island.

Then, whooping and brandishing weapons, a band of Indians defended the mock burning of a Sauk village and young braves staged a big hunting party. One of the major events was the dedication of the replica of the old Fort Armstrong blockhouse, which still stands today on the island. On Pioneer and Pageant Day, a special pageant was enacted on the island's main avenue.

The whole avenue was electrically illuminated. Depicted in allegorical form was the area's progress since the establishment of Fort Armstrong. The following day, a massive parade, marked by many floats, passed through Quad-City streets, and historical pageantry was again staged on the island. The night was devoted to a pyrotechnical display of "Old Mexico" in Rock Island's Exposition Park.

The next day was dubbed "Industrial and Fraternal Day." After military maneuvers were conducted on the island, 100,000 members of industrial and fraternal organizations paraded through area downtown streets. Most business houses and factories closed for the day so their members could participate. The night's activities featured a spectacular water carnival.

On the last day of the celebration, "Young American Day" was observed, with members of Sunday School organizations, Boy Scouts and others marching behind bands in a big parade. No one could doubt, when it was all over, that the old fort's 100th birthday had been celebrated in unsurpassed style. □

2nd Street looking east from Harrison, about 1918. Davenport, Iowa.

Third and Brady Sts., Davenport, Iowa.

DAVENPORT'S 'SPACE' SHOT

America's first "entry" into the space race possibly occurred in Davenport, on a still morning way back on Feb. 12, 1917. Nobody planned it that way, but when the boiler blew at the old Woolen Mill near East River Street and College Avenue it set some sort of record, locally at least.

Everything appeared to be all right at 2 a.m. when foreman Roy Gidley on his nightly rounds made a cursory examination of the steam pressure on the boiler. The gauge stood at 80 pounds, right where she belonged, he noted.

It looked like just another long, uneventful night in the mill, Gidley thought as he leaned against a door jamb and watched engineer Ray Carroll prepare to start the motor the boilers operated. Thinking of other things, Gidley glanced idly at the big, 48-inch upright boiler and was amazed to see wisps of steam wafting lazily from the top. He looked closer and observed that the seams appeared to be swelling.

Strange, Gidley thought, and to the engineer he said, "What's the matter with your boiler, Ray?"

One look was enough for the engineer. He screamed, "I'm going!" and dove through the door. Gidley was right behind him and kept up, even though he had a lame leg. The two men had no sooner passed through the door when the boiler blew with a shuddering blast that shook the homes for blocks around.

The door was ripped off its hinges and knocked down one of the fleeing men. All about them flew pieces of glass, brick and smashed wooden beams. Almost immediately, an inverted cone of fire and smoke billowed from the building. Baffled residents for blocks around found their homes engulfed in a rain of bricks, glass and assorted debris. Shooting upward like a rocket, the boiler crashed through two floors and tore through the roof. Upward it went, higher and higher, and when the boiler was several hundred feet in the air, witnesses heard another loud blast as its head blew off, producing an effect somewhat similar to that of a two-stage rocket.

When it finally came down, the huge boiler crashed on a sidewalk on College Avenue, a full 800 feet away. Engineers estimated that to have traveled that far the boiler must have reached a height of almost one mile in its upward curve. It crashed with such force that the concrete was driven six inches into the ground and the imprint of the boiler and its pipes was left on the sidewalk.

But the boiler still hadn't lost its momentum. It caromed across the street, snapping off a six-inch tree a foot above the ground. It finally stopped just short of a home at 211 College Avenue. A piece of the boiler head, which had fallen off when it blew up in mid-flight, plowed into the roof of a home a block away, blasting a hole three-feet in diameter before stopping in the attic.

The terrific concussion broke windows in many nearby homes, and falling bricks tore holes in roofs. In the mill itself, a number of new tables and 500 yards of new leather were destroyed. The center of the building, where the boiler had been, was gutted. Damage was estimated at $15,000, a large sum in those times. Many nearby buildings suffered fire and smoke damage.

Many Davenporters, seeing the rising pillar of fire and smoke from a distance, thought the Rock Island Arsenal, then turning out weapons for World War I, was on fire. Only the fact the explosion occurred at such an early hour when the normally busy streets were empty, saved a probable loss of life. The two men, who had been in the building at the time of the blast, managed to escape.

Firemen fought hard to save the building, but the flames spread too quickly. Too, it was bitterly cold, and water poured on the building froze to ice almost immediately. The entire area was soon one giant icicle. A street car froze to a nearby track and it took an hour's work with blowtorches to free it.

The force of the explosion could be gauged by the fact a bolt two inches in diameter and almost a foot long was found imbedded in the trunk of a tree a half block away from the woolen mills. Davenport's unscheduled "rocket launch" could hardly be termed a success. □

MUSIC, DANCING ABOARD THE COLORFUL EXCURSION BOATS

The big, white paddlewheel dipped and splashed as the steamboat "St. Paul," venerable "daddy of 'em all," lazed upstream in the glorious, by-gone days of the Mississippi River.

Booming out across the muddy, moonlit waters was the solid Dixie beat of "High Society," so high and sweet it was already luring crowds from the villages to the river banks.

There was, however, nothing sweet or serene about the mien of Capt. Joe Streckfus, master of the St. Paul, and owner of the growing line of steamboats that bore his name.

"Get that idiot off the bandstand. If he's too damn bashful to stand up and sing instead of blowing that horn, get him clear off the boat," boomed the leather-lunged captain.

That "poor, shy, idiot" who seemed to have reached the end of his embryonic career right in mid-river, one day would overcome his timidity, and joyous crowds from Arkansas to Zanzibar would cheer the name and the golden horn of Louis (Satchmo) Armstrong.

Capt. Joe, whose home town was Rock Island, Ill., was a martinet when it involved the manner in which music was played aboard the Streckfus excursion boats, and he had a direct hand in molding the careers of many fine and famous musicians.

He wasn't always right, though. He once threatened to fire the whole band if they didn't get rid of one cornet player. To Streckfus' mind the man had

The excursion steamer, St. Paul, during one of its many river cruises. (Buffalo Bill Museum Collection.)

one unforgivable sin—he couldn't read music. For that reason, Capt. Joe finally banned the young man — and his horn — from both the steamboats "Capitol" and "Washington."

The snub, though, didn't stop the young man from playing. He went on to gain immortality and make the name Bix Beiderbecke a standard of musical excellence and genius.

The late Capt. C.W. Elder of Moline, Ill. was once a musician aboard the famed Streckfus boats, and knew both Capt. Joe and his brother, Capt. John Streckfus, well.

Excursion steamers St. Paul, Silver Crescent, and J.S. at Davenport, Iowa in the early part of this century. (A & A Coins, Stamps, and Collectables.)

Elder recalled what a musical taskmaster Capt. Joe was. He left nothing to chance and would invariably attend rehearsals, tapping his feet with his watch in his hand. Woe to someone if the band failed to keep the proper tempo — 70 beats a minute for fox trots, and 90 for one-steps. If it happened too often, there were bound to be new faces aboard.

Despite his strictness, Capt. Joe gave many fledgling musicians their start. He insisted upon regular rehearsals and always strove for perfection. "Dixieland" music, of course, was born in New Orleans, but it was Streckfus steamboats that carried the happy sound upriver from the bayou country, and made devotees of those in the north who heard it.

The new music was an instant hit in the north. Elder recalled how huge crowds would throng about the steamboat "Sidney," the first real excursion craft to go upriver. One of the siren sounds that lured

them was the playing of Fate Marable who Elder called "By far the most colorful river boat musician in the country." Marable played an air calliope in the boat's ballroom and the rollicking sounds rolled out across the river. "Satchmo" Armstrong was one of Marable's proteges.

Other graduates of the "Streckfus-Marable School" included trumpet man Charles Creath, and Dewey Jackson, both of whom later led their own bands and made recordings; and bassman Jimmy Blanton, later a featured soloist with Duke Ellington. Others included George (Pops) Foster and Arthur James (Zutty) Singleton.

Each prospective clarinet player on a Streckfus boat had to pass one all-important test. "High Society" was one of Capt. Joe's favorites, and if the musician could play that, the captain figured he could play anything.

Elder said the original Dixieland Band, the actual start of the Northward movement, was composed in 1913 of Nick LaRoca, cornet; George Brunis, trombone; Anton Lada, drums, and Harry Ragas, piano. Though many other lines tried, none could compare with the quality of "Dixieland" music served up aboard the Streckfus boats.

Elder related, "On Streckfus boats the laggards couldn't help but improve, what with the coaching of the leader and Capt. Joe. They either got good, or else dropped out. The hours were terrible with the long all-day trips and moonlights. In later years Capt. Joe was obliged to use two bands; one for the day trips (smaller) and a big band for the evening. On tramping trips all bands played until their members were unconscious."

Standard Dixie tunes included "Dixieland One Step," "Millenburg Joys," "High Society," "Panama," "Clarinet Marmalade," "At the Jazz Band Ball," and "Muscat Ramble." Many times, captains begged the bands to slow the tempo because they feared the dancing crowds would tear the boats apart.

A colorful era died when the last riverboat band was stilled forever. □

BUGGING THE MAYOR'S OFFICE

The controversy over "bugging" offices and telephones of persons suspected of wrong-doing still rages in the United States today and is the subject of much legal study, but as long ago as 1921, shocked Davenporters learned that a hidden listening device had been concealed in no less a place than their mayor's office in City Hall.

The strange "bugging" device might have gone undetected, had not Mayor Dr. C.L. Barewald leaned back in the big chair in his office and stared ceilingward as he pondered some weighty municipal problem.

Something else was vaguely bothering him, something about the chandelier that hung directly above his desk. "The chandelier...hmmm? Wait a minute, there appeared to be finger marks in the dust that had accumulated for years and years. Now why would anyone have been up there fiddling around with that light fixture?"

Picking up his phone, Mayor Barewald summoned Charles Boettcher, his chief of police. The chief looked at the marks in the dust and stood on a chair to peer over the top of the chandelier. Then he whistled, and said in a very surprised voice, "just look at this, Mayor."

Affixed to a bronze ball that was part of the decoration was a transmitter of the type used on dictaphone machines. The two men traced the wires up through tubing in the base of the chandelier.

The significance of the find stunned Mayor Barewald. Here was evidence of a sinister plot. Two detectives were called immediately and ordered to trace the hidden wires to a recording device that almost certainly had to be hidden somewhere. The wires seemed to lead through the tubing to the fourth floor, which was a garret used as a storeroom. The detectives no sooner reached the fourth floor stairs than they encountered the city electrician. He blurted that he was fixing the motor of the City Hall clock.

2nd Street looking east from Harrison, Davenport, Iowa.

Ordering the electrician to stay where he was, the detectives continued to trace the wires which they found eventually connected with a heavily insulated cable. The cable, in turn, twisted under boxes and bales of rubble to the receiving end directly below the City Hall tower.

The cable ended in two contact points, but detectives could find no receiving device attached to the wires. Under the pile of rubbish, though, the officers located a receiver attached to two dry cell batteries. Someone obviously had intended to listen in on conversations in the mayor's office. But who? And why?

Detectives returned to the electrician and questioned him. He told several conflicting stories, but finally confessed that he had installed the "bug" on orders of one of the Socialist Party aldermen on the city council.

Strangely enough, the alderman readily admitted his part in the plot, but declined further comment on advice of his attorney. In the uproar that followed disclosure of the scheme, many citizens cried that it was a plan to discredit the mayor, and no doubt involved the whole Socialist Party in the city. Detectives said they had found evidence linking the "Frantic Five," as some called the Socialist aldermen, to the bugging incident. This charge was vehemently denied.

Then there was another twist. The city electrician who had installed the device and the alderman who had ordered it, began hinting that they had "something on" the mayor and the chief of police as a result of their eavesdropping. The electrician then made another startling admission. He said a similar listening device had been hidden for some time in the chief's office.

Mayor Barewald had been elected along with the Socialist aldermen, but within a year bolted the party, declaring his former colleagues blocked conservative measures in every way. The alderman who admitted ordering the bugging said that since Mayor Barewald's decision, his party had discovered the city had "opened up." He said he was attempting to gather evidence that the major and chief had "offered protection" to unlawful elements.

The electrician claimed the device in the mayor's office had been in operation for a week, but when police tested it, they found it worked poorly. Claiming attempts at intimidation, Chief Boettcher declared, "Let them come ahead with their charges if they think they have anything!"

Mayor Barewald also protested his innocence of any wrong-doing and wanted to bring criminal charges against both men, but County Attorney John Weir said he could find no grounds for charges of conspiracy against either man because "intent" could not be established.

He did say it was possible the electrician could be charged with violating the building code by running telephone wires through the same tubing that contained light wires. The mayor later appeared at the closing of the Dr. Jim Kramer revival meetings at Calvary Baptist Church. In addition to repeating he had done nothing wrong, he declared that he loved the flag and was a true American.

The mayor was still determined to bring charges against his tormentors, and hired his own attorney. He could not use the services of the city attorney because that man was representing the alderman who had ordered the bugging.

The Socialists held a series of rather frantic meetings, and on Jan. 30 strongly denied any knowledge of the bugging. They termed it "a childish act without reason." For weeks the charges and counter-charges and threats flew back and forth, but eventually a truce was called and no charges were filed.

Barewald ran for mayor again the next term, this time on the Democratic ticket, but the people of Davenport apparently had had enough and he wasn't reelected. □

REBIRTH OF THE FATHER OF WATERS

Never in the palmy days of the steamboat was the Mississippi River as mighty as it is today. Up and down the giant waterway go the products of farm and factory. Yearly the river's economic impact becomes greater upon the cities along its banks. Giant factories, some employing atomic power, are locating next to it.

This rebirth of river shipping, dealt a death blow by the railroads, and the fact that much of it was unnavigable in the early 1900s, began when the various locks and dams were completed.

Delta Queen seen from Prairie Du Chien, Wisconsin.

In its natural condition the river was navigable for light-draft boats as far upstream as St. Paul in times of normal flow. River travel, however, was restricted at times of low water. On the upper river, two rapids, one at Rock Island, Ill., and the other at the mouth of the Des Moines River below Keokuk, Iowa, caused extreme trouble.

Authorization of four-and-a-half, and later six foot channels on the Upper Mississippi didn't solve the navigation difficulties. By 1930, river traffic had dwindled to a scant 527,000 tons a year. The Rock Island lock and dam was the first of 26 completed and in operation on the river by 1939, along with a uniform nine-foot channel. The locks and dams provided a veritable "stairway of water" 658 miles long for commercial and recreational boat traffic.

Tugboat going through the lock at the Government Bridge, Davenport, Iowa.

Marina at Lansing, Iowa.

Shippers were quick to take advantage of this most economical way to transport huge cargoes, and the Mississippi lived again, eventually stronger than ever before. The revival of river shipping has meant a cheaper way for people to get their products to market and to obtain the raw materials needed for production. It has meant new grain processing plants, chemical factories, and river terminals, and naturally more jobs and more money flowing into the river communities. River terminals now average one for every 45 miles of channel, and more are being built each year.

Recreational boating has undergone a tremendous increase, with small boat harbors springing up all along the river. Often the hey-day of the Mississippi is thought of as about the Civil War time when it's estimated 1,100 steamboats were traveling the Upper Mississippi. Yet in a typical season in 1866, records show 917 steamboats passed through St. Louis with barges carrying a total of 377,804 tons of goods. Compare that with the many millions of tons carried today!

Petroleum products, grain and coal are three of the principle products shipped by barge on the Upper Mississippi, with petroleum the largest single

View of the river with boat, Upper Mississippi.

View from Pikes Peak.

tonnage product. Oil terminals are located in many places along the river. Tanker trucks pick up the water-delivered fuel and take it inland. Many of the electric power plants along the river receive all of their coal by barge, but no perishable products can be shipped by barge due to the relatively slow speed of towboats.

Today's towboats are a far cry from those of yesteryear. Modern towboats have up to 3,200 horsepower, or more, and are powered by diesel engines. They average 150 feet long, 35 feet wide, and draw about nine feet of water. A coal tow today may haul 20,000 tons, or the equivalent of three full train loads. A petroleum tow may haul 4,500,000 gallons, which would fill 563 railroad tank cars, or 600 trailer trucks. The inland towboat fleet is double the number of American flag vessels operating today on the seven seas and the Great Lakes combined.

The experts say there is every indication traffic on the big river will grow even heavier, especially if it is found feasible to keep it open for year-around navigation. Studies aimed at determining this possibility are now underway. □

SARCOPHAGUS OF SAND

I throw fistfuls of coarse
grained sand
at ants
smearing the shore.
They move toward algae,
toward silver skeleton fish,
river water flotsam—
lying on their sides,
a cemetery
of sun-worshippers:
decapitated souls streak the channel
as wind blows up.

Minnows, golden slivers of light
gyrate beyond shore stones,
circling the spikes of trees
like offshore pirates,
they swim to survive
an eternity of silt.
The current buries them
under a wildwood barge.

Poem and photograph by Sue Katz, Rock Island, Ill.

Photo by Sue Katz, Rock Island, Ill.

JIM ARPY

Mr. Arpy has been a feature writer and columnist for the Quad-City Times, Davenport, Iowa, since 1951. Born in San Pedro, California, he graduated from Drake University with a degree in Journalism. He is a veteran of World War II.

"As I have conducted historical 'detective work', I have been constantly impressed with the Mississippi Valley area and continually dismayed to learn how few people are aware of its importance and heritage."

This book was born from his intense interest in the area's history and from exhaustive research into little known historical facts. □

JOHN M. ZIELINSKI

Mr. Zielinski is an extremely active writer/photographer. In addition to his best selling "Portrait of Iowa," he has also published a number of successful books. Among them "Amish Across America", "Iowa Barn Book No. 1", "Mesquakie and Proud of It", and "Portrait of Iowa Travel Guide". His work has also appeared in the Chicago Tribune, Kansas City Star, and San Francisco Chronicle. John works out of Iowa City, Iowa. □

These are some of the cities and towns that played roles, large or small, in the history and development of the lands along the Magnificent Mississippi:

ILLINOIS

Rock Island, Moline, East Moline, Beardstown, Oquawka, Prophetstown, Dixon, Quincy, Kellogg's Grove, Galena, Port Byron, Nauvoo, Alton, Geneseo, Atkinson, Springfield, Chicago, Andalusia, Hampton, Bishop Hill, Cambridge and Kaskaskia.

IOWA

Davenport, Bettendorf, Keokuk, Selma, Lexington, Burlington, LeClaire, Dubuque, Muscatine, Bellevue, Fort Atkinson, Iowa City, Cedar Falls, Clinton, Cedar Rapids, Council Bluffs, Des Moines, Mt. Pleasant, Fairfield, Ottumwa, Oskaloosa, Keosauqua, Andrew, Fort Madison, McCausland, Buffalo, Buena Vista and Amana.

OTHER CITIES

Big Dells, WI; Jefferson Barracks, MO; St. Louis MO; Kahokia, MO; Prairie du Chien, WI; Minneapolis, MN; Nashville, TN; New Orleans, LA; Boston, MA; New York, NY; Washington, DC; St. Paul, MN; Casper, WY; Rock Creek, WY; Salt Lake City, UT; Cody, WY; Harper's Ferry, VA; Arlington, VA; Charleston, SC; Helena, AR; Winona, MN; and Hastings, MN.

□